This Book Belongs to

MERRY CHRISTMAS

Color Test

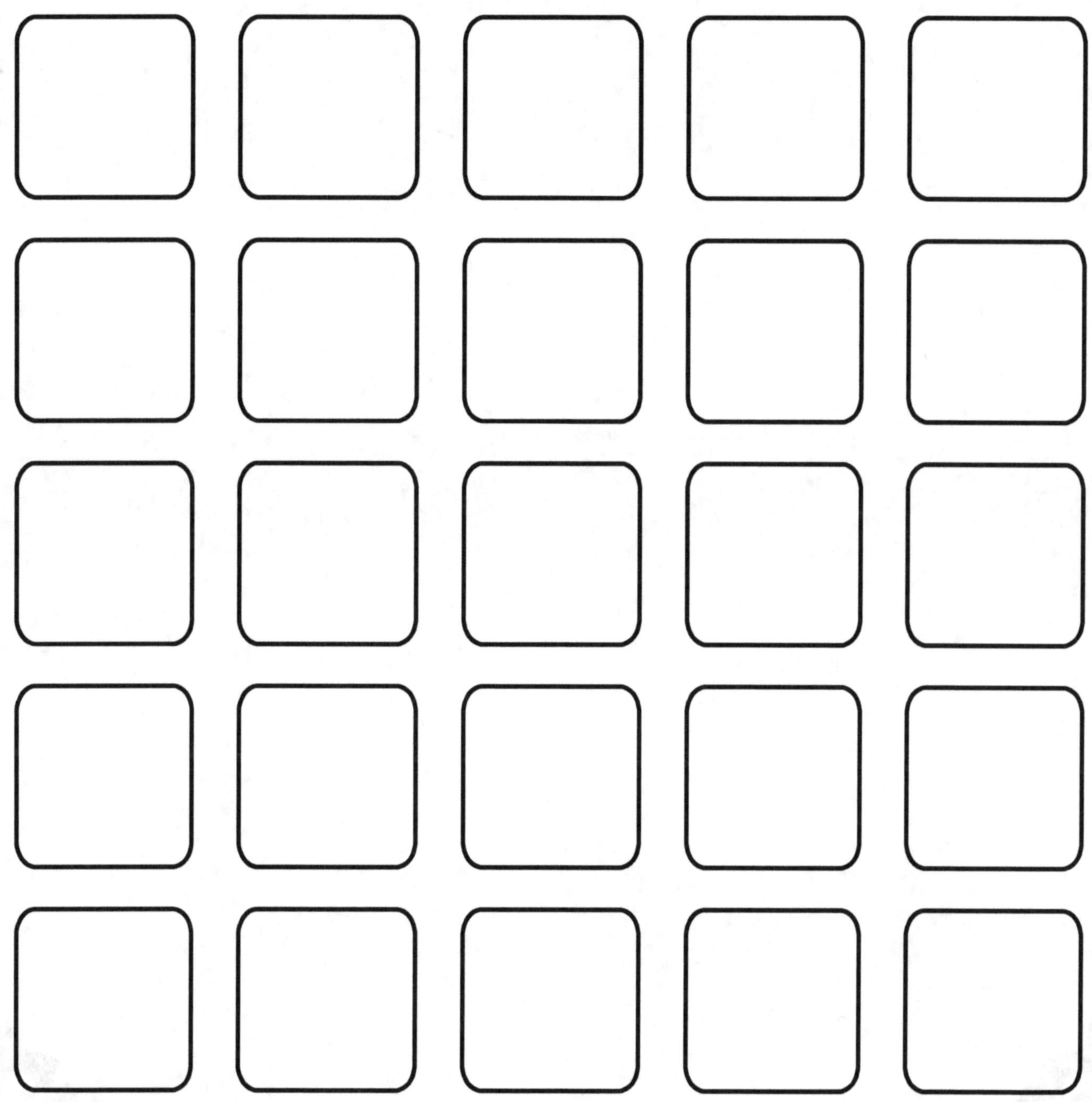

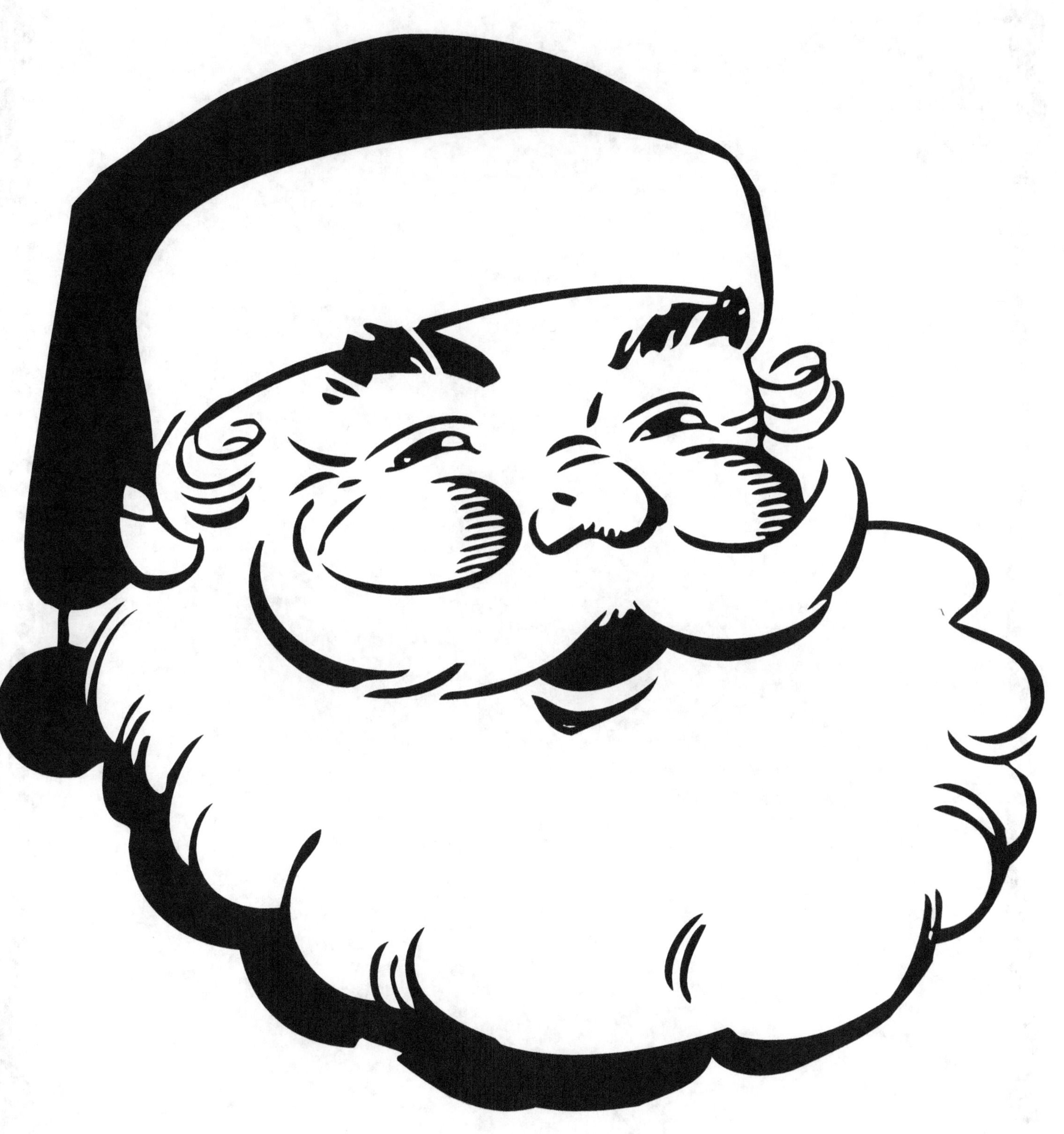

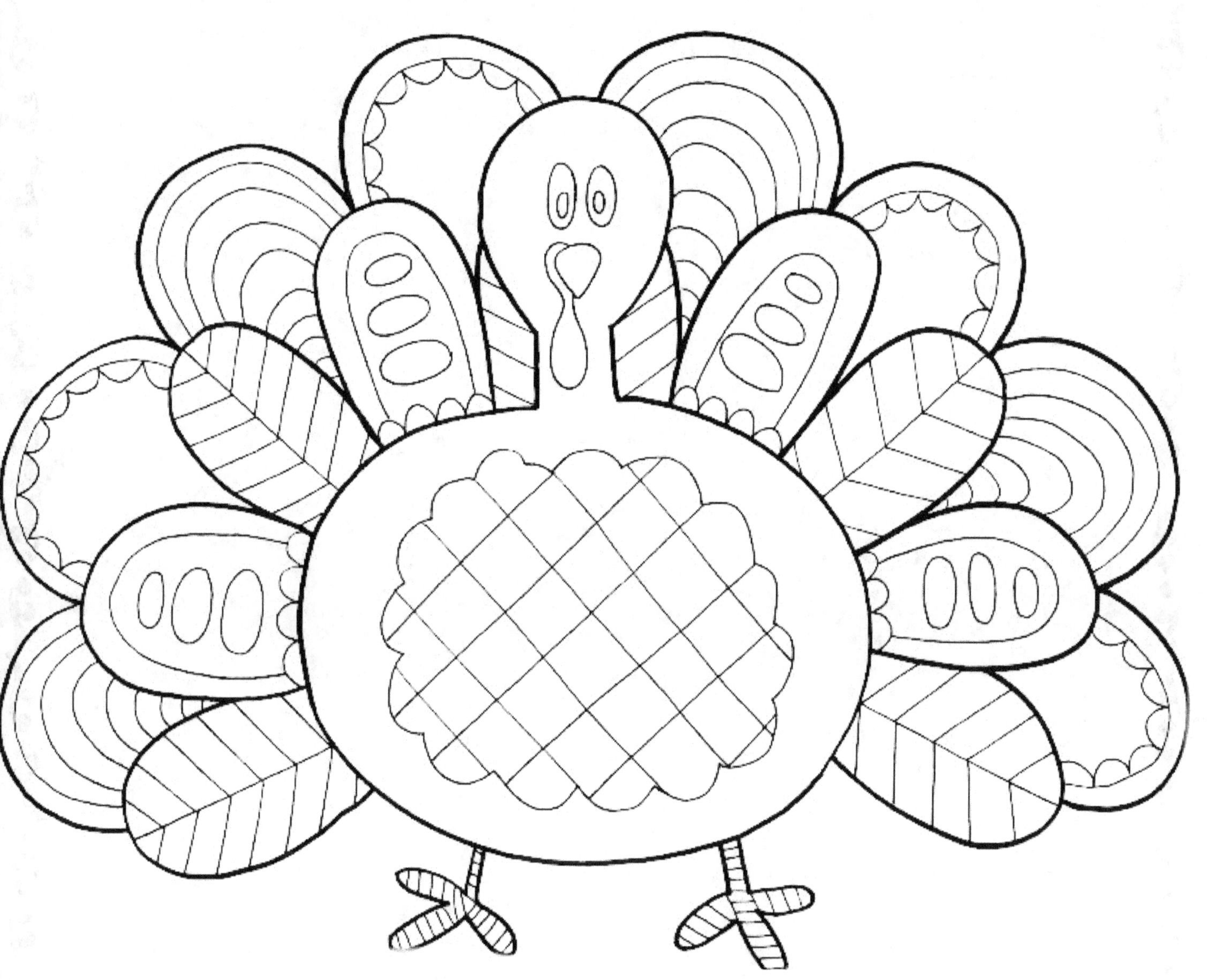

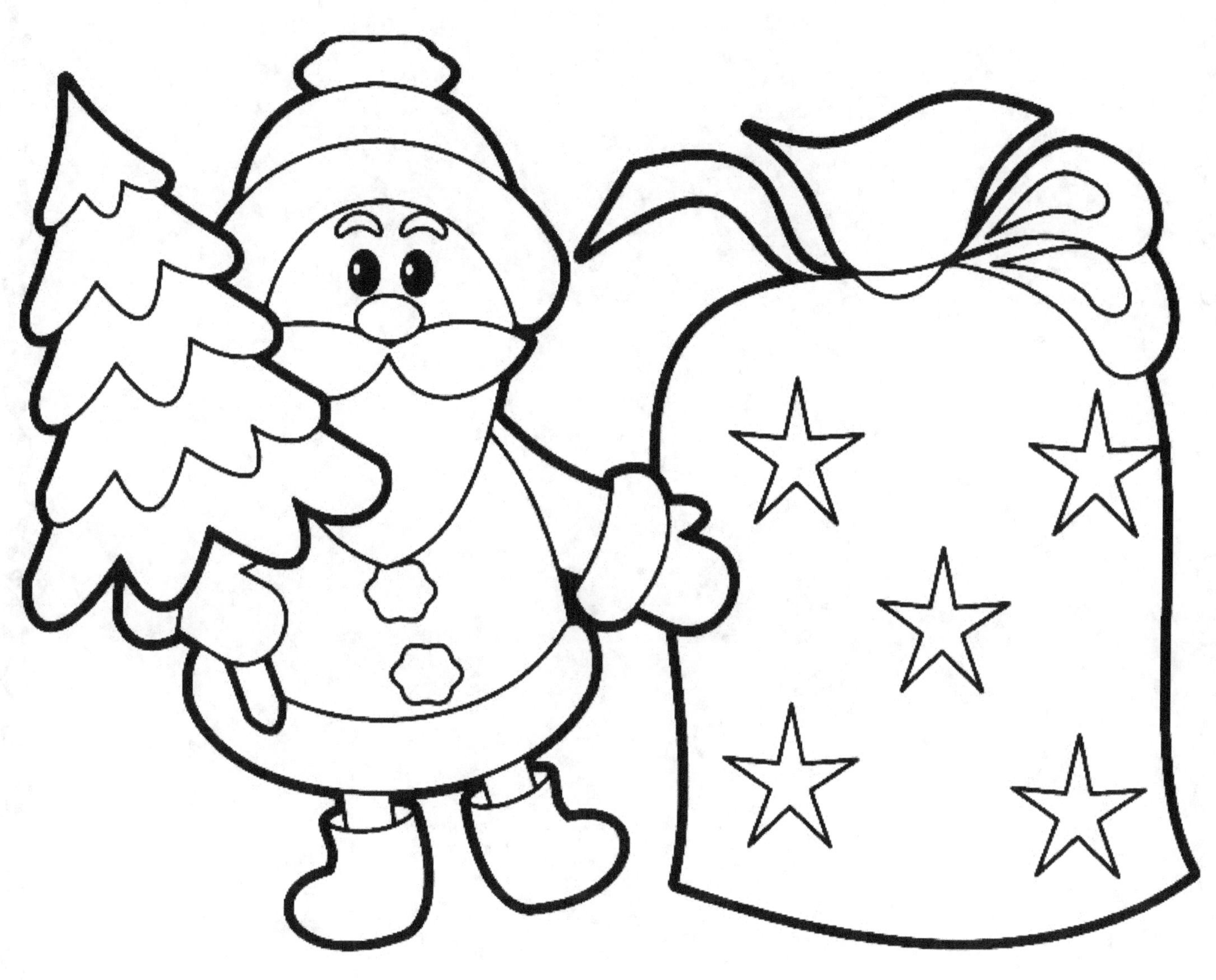

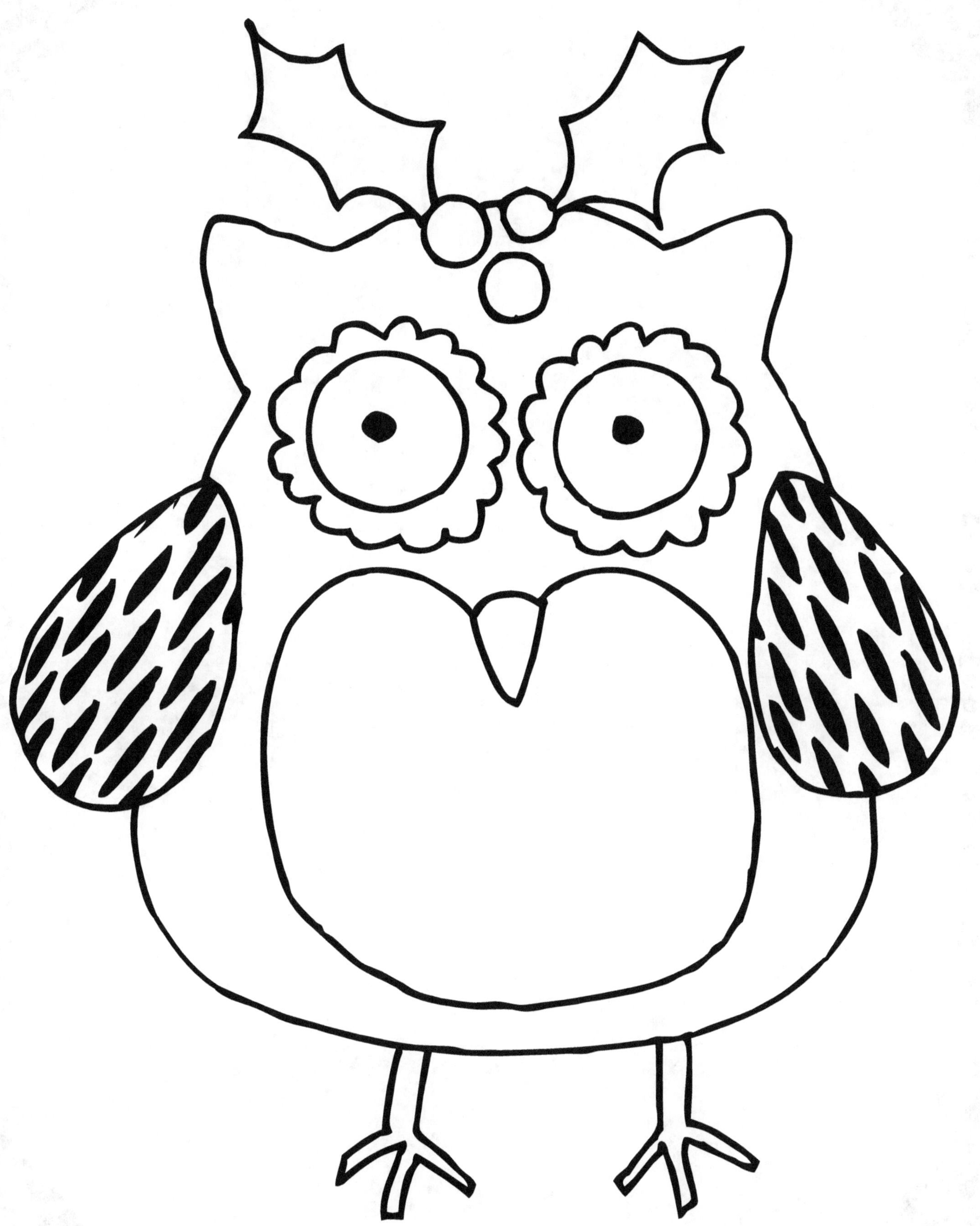

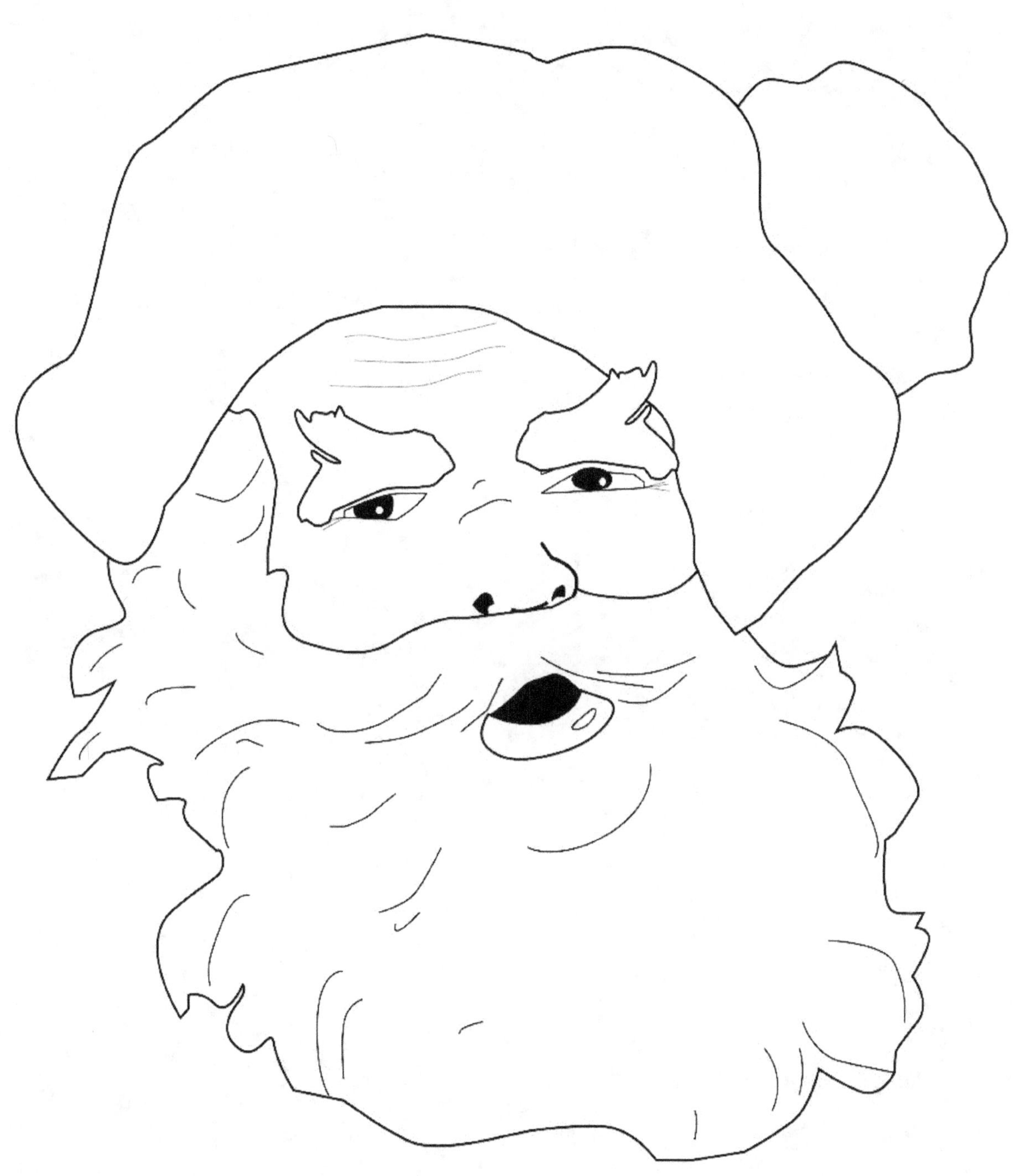

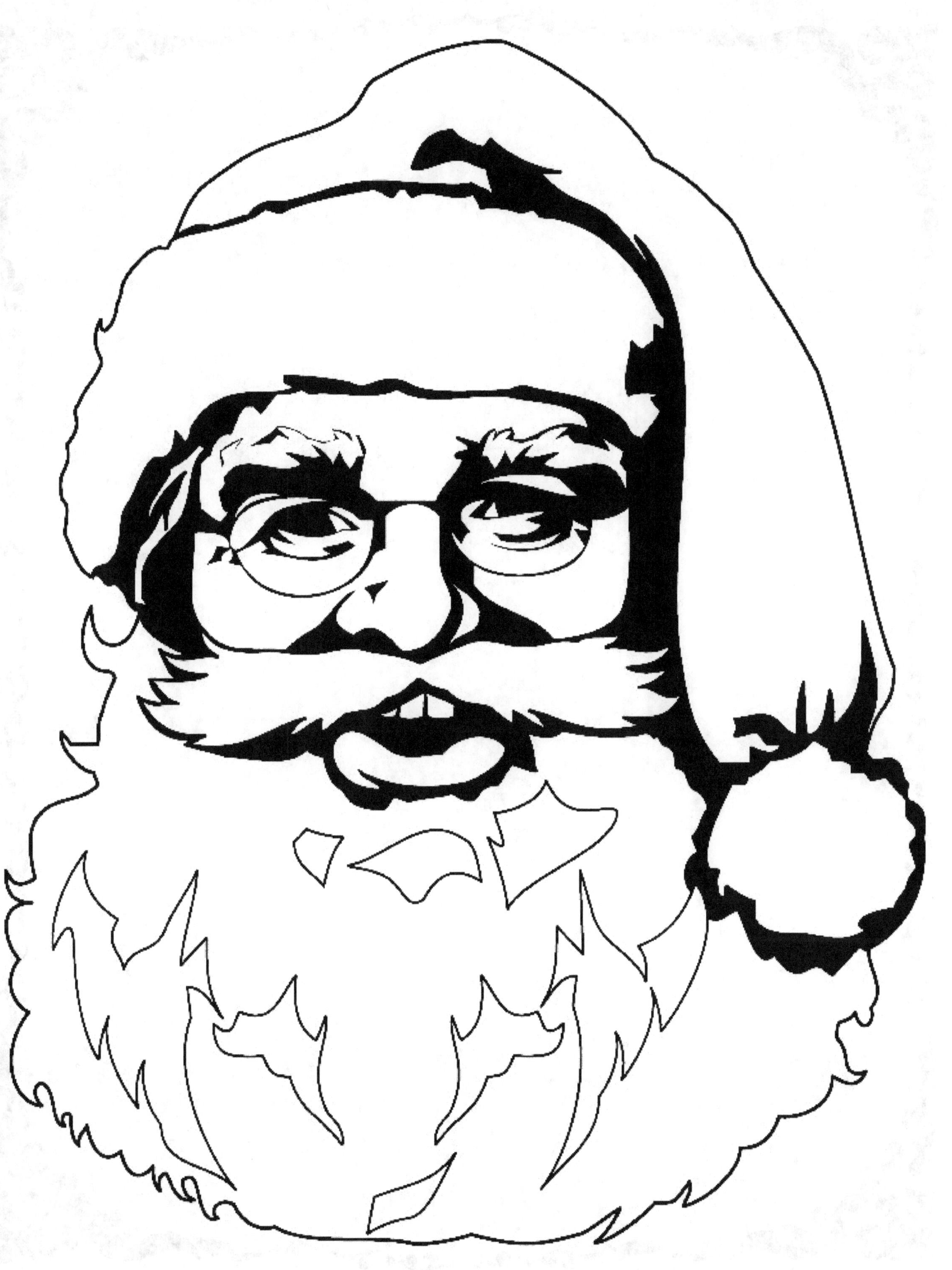

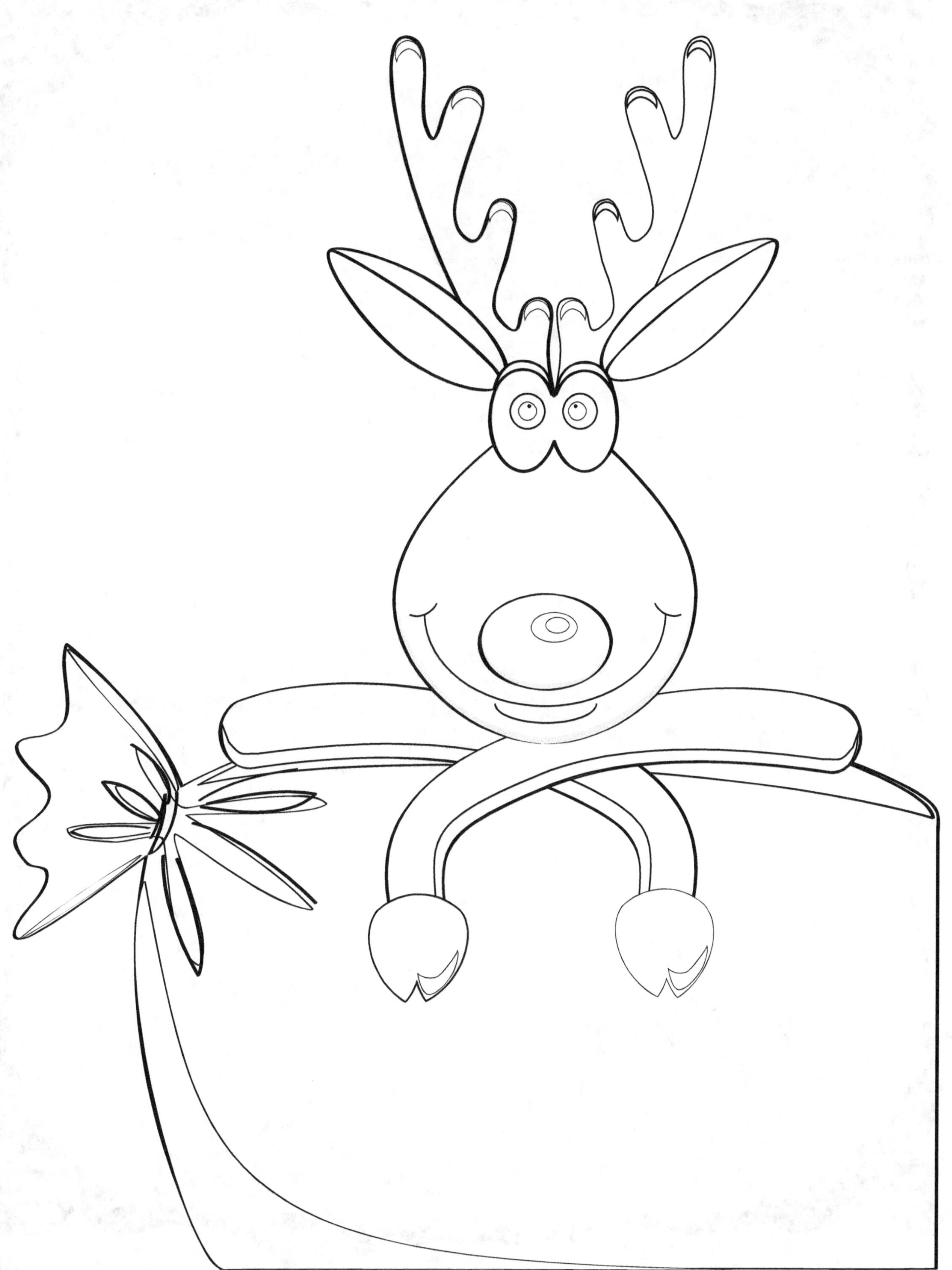

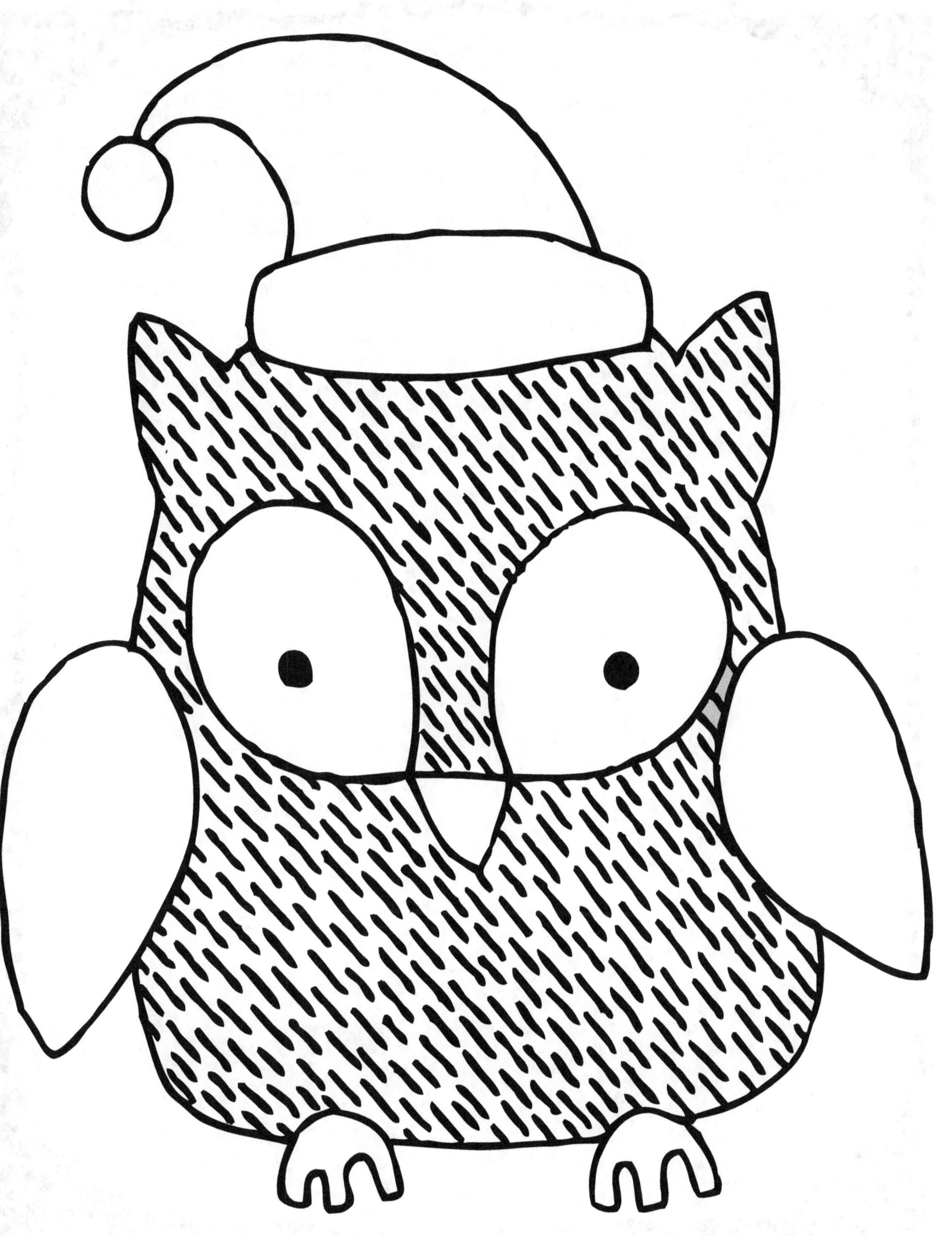

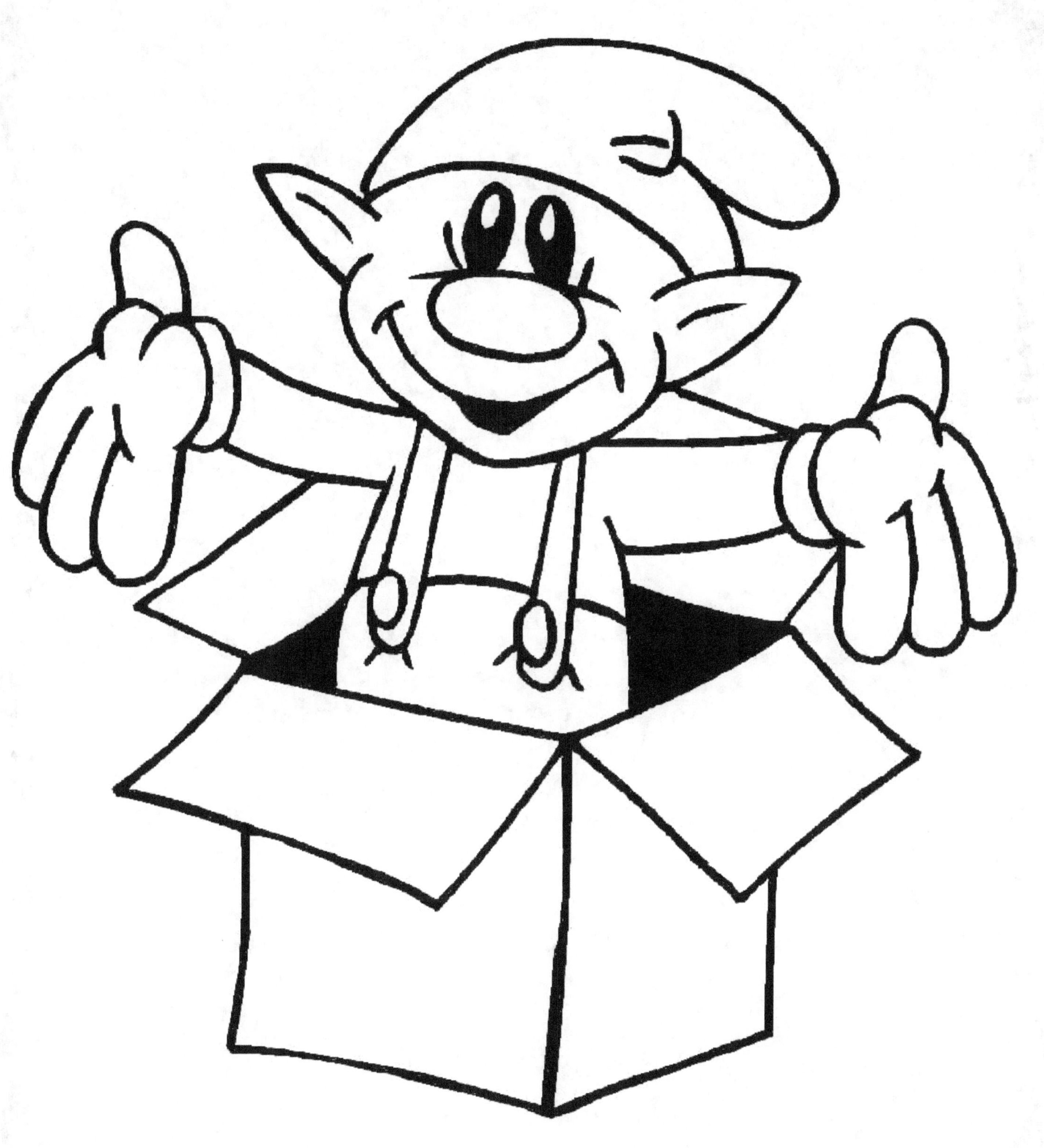

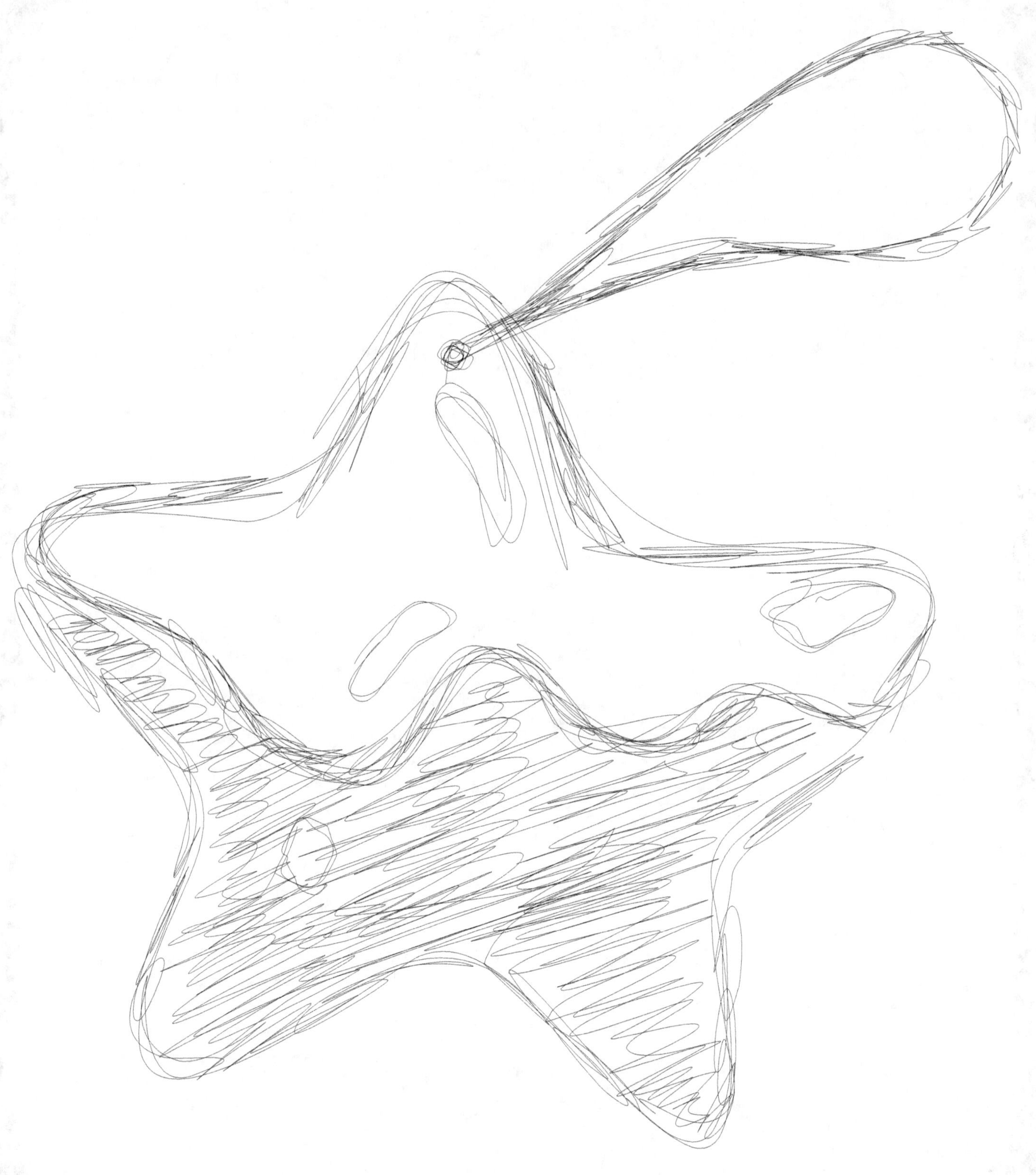

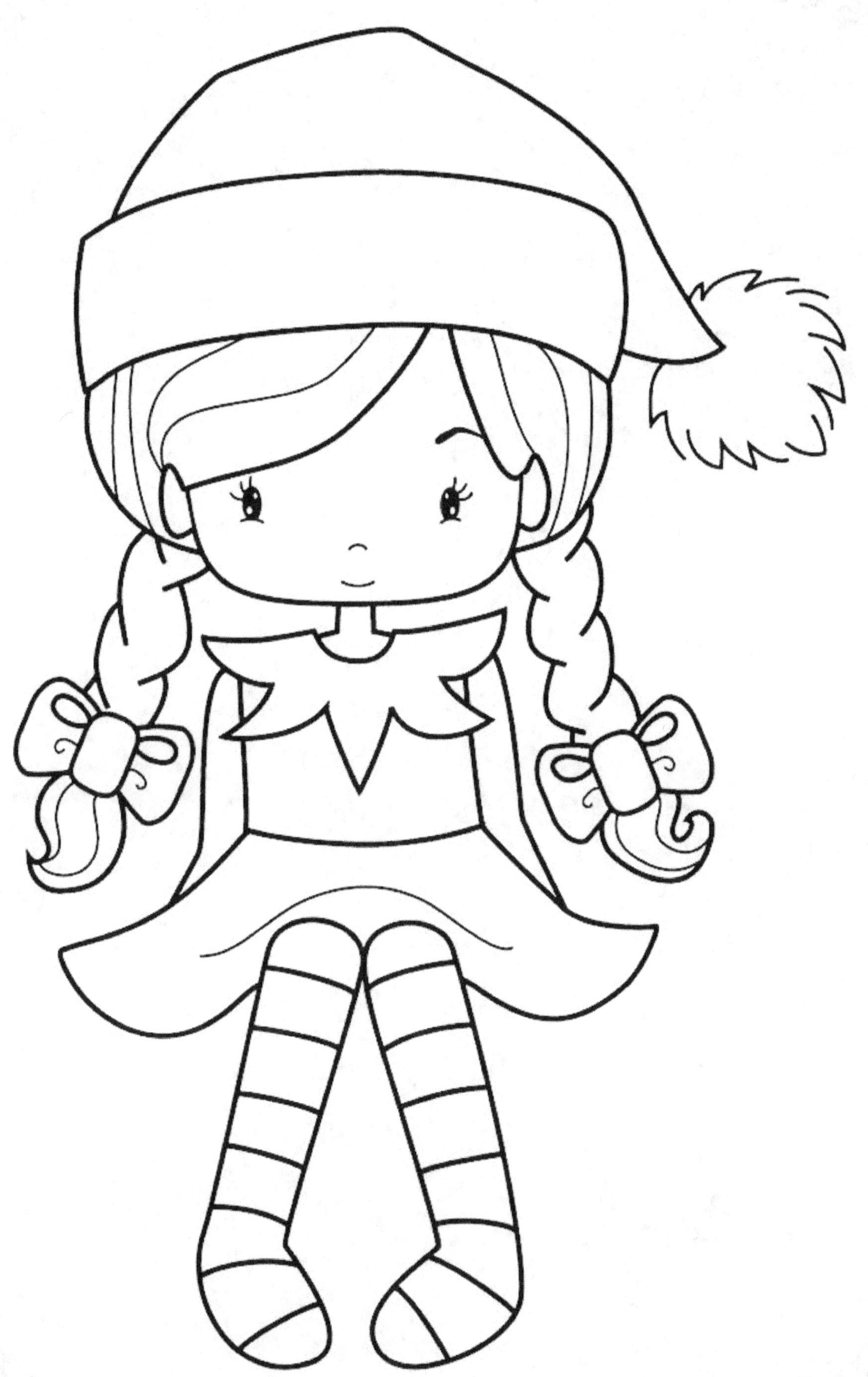

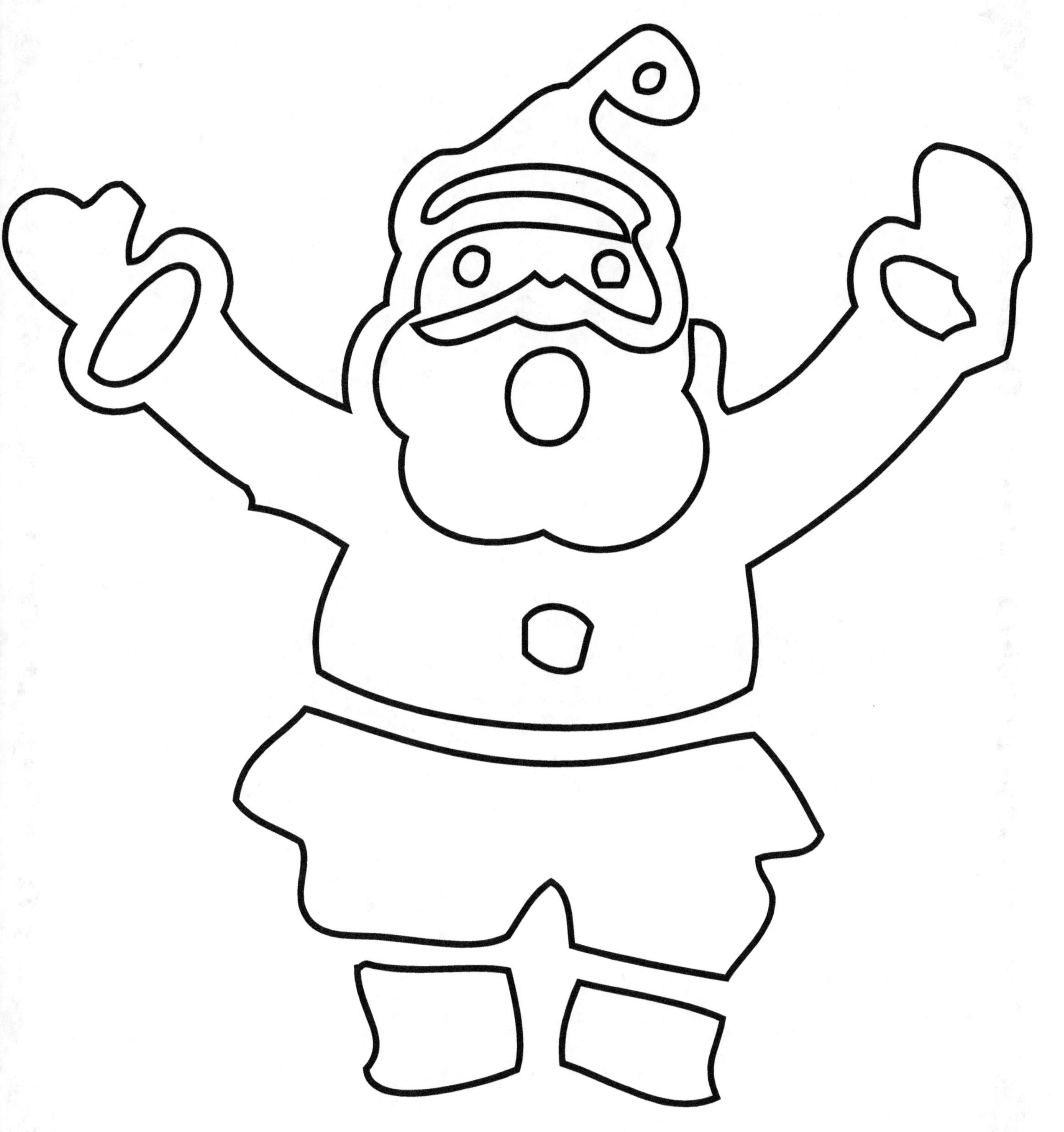

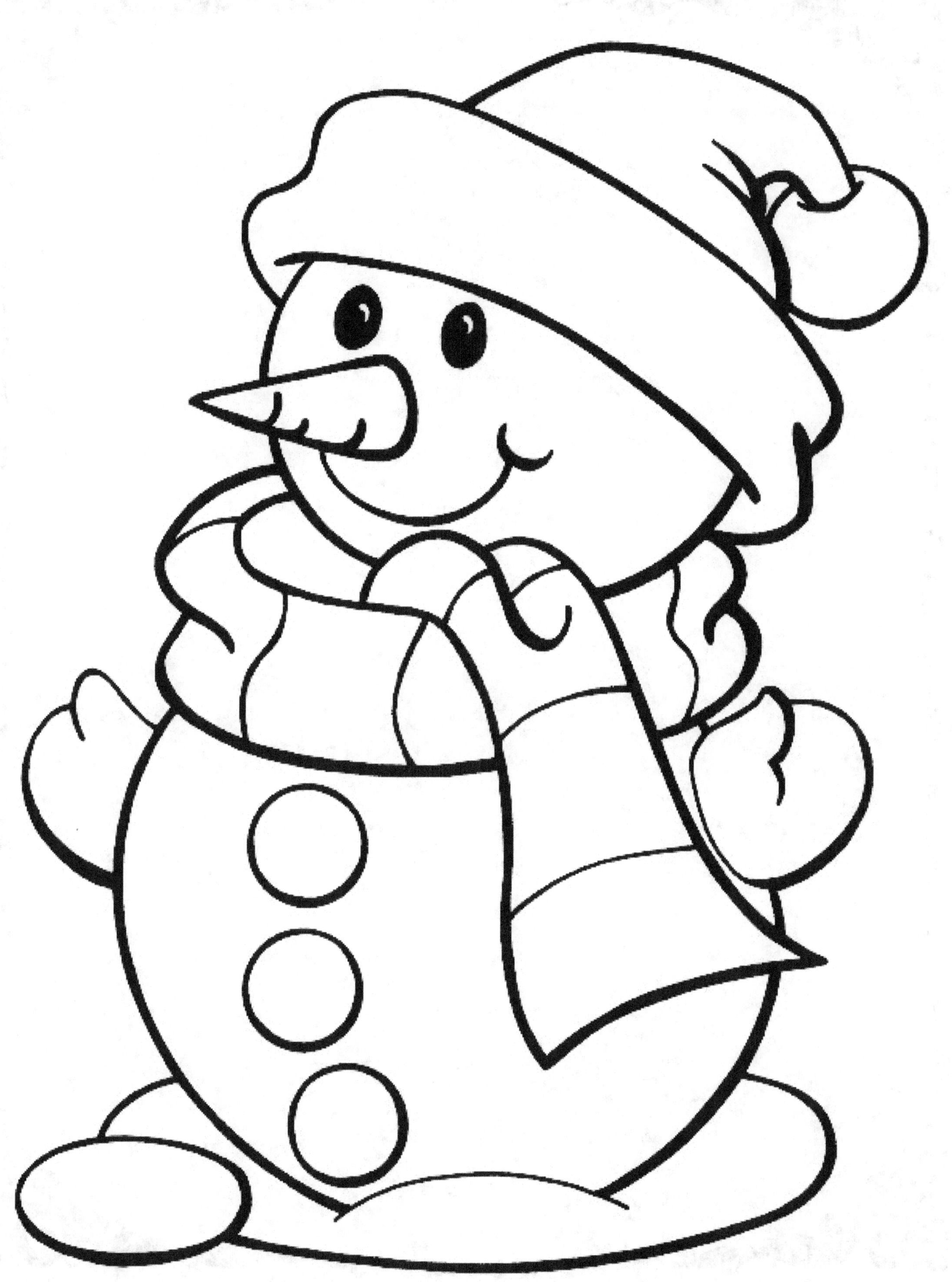

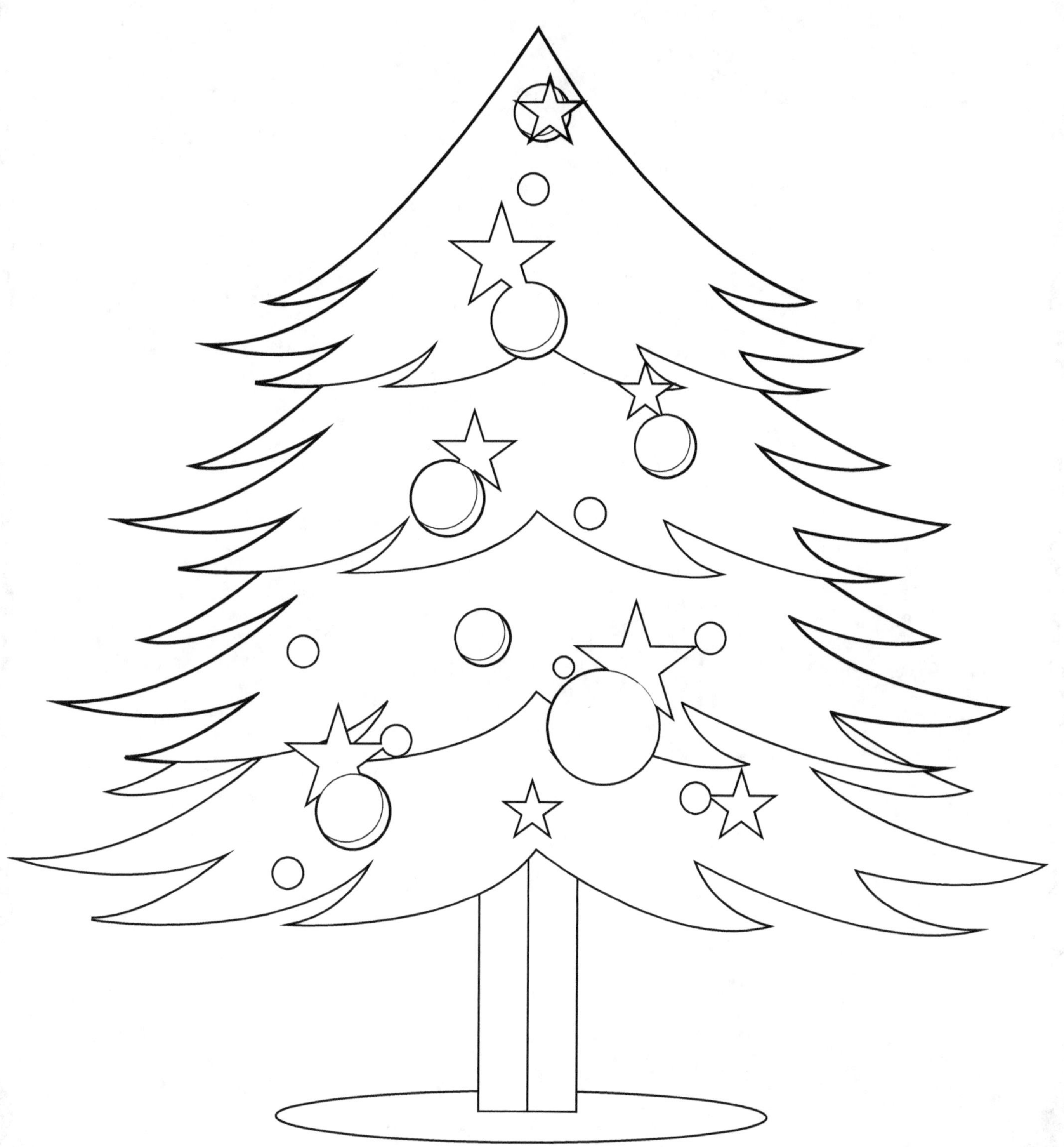

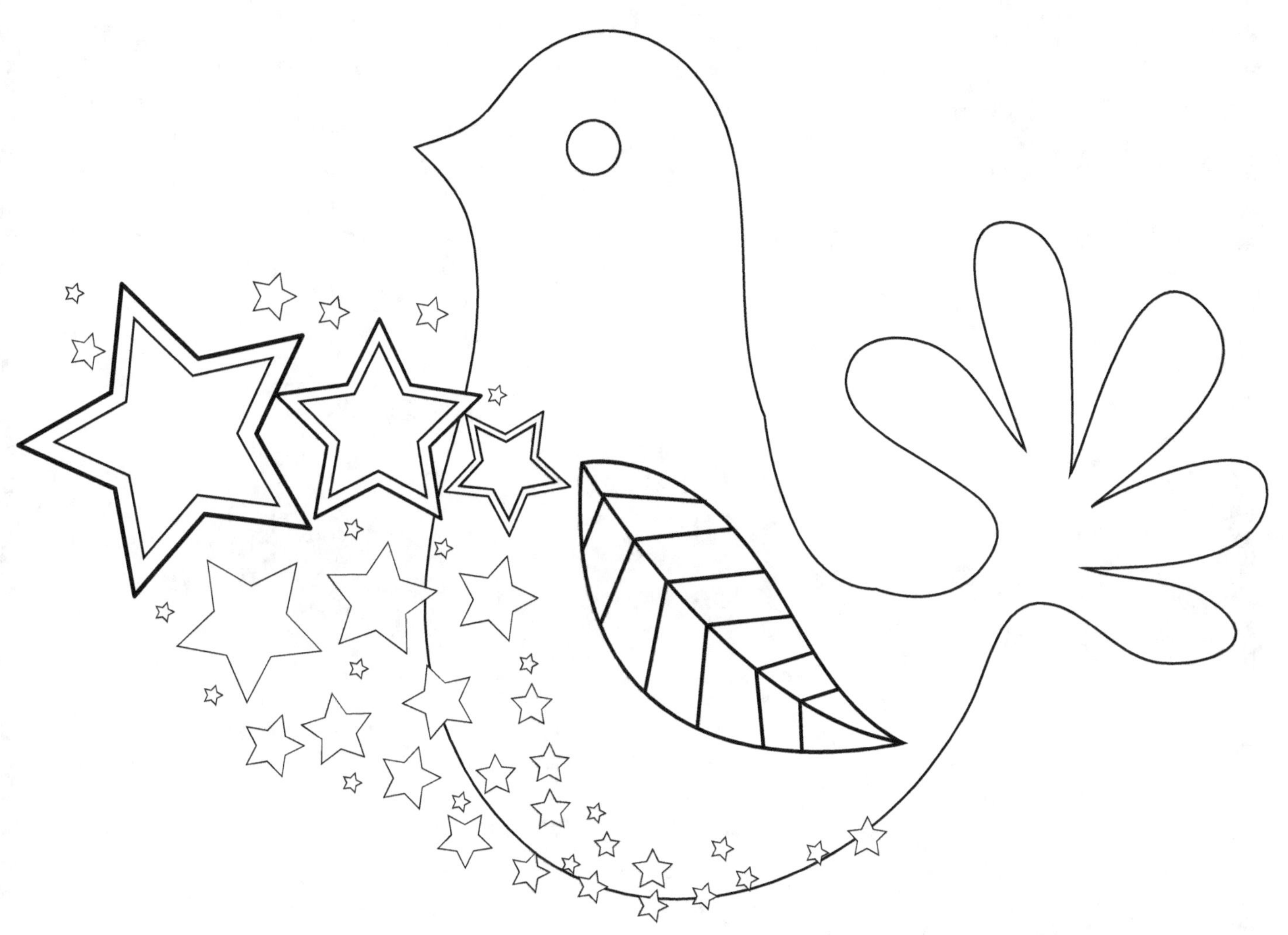

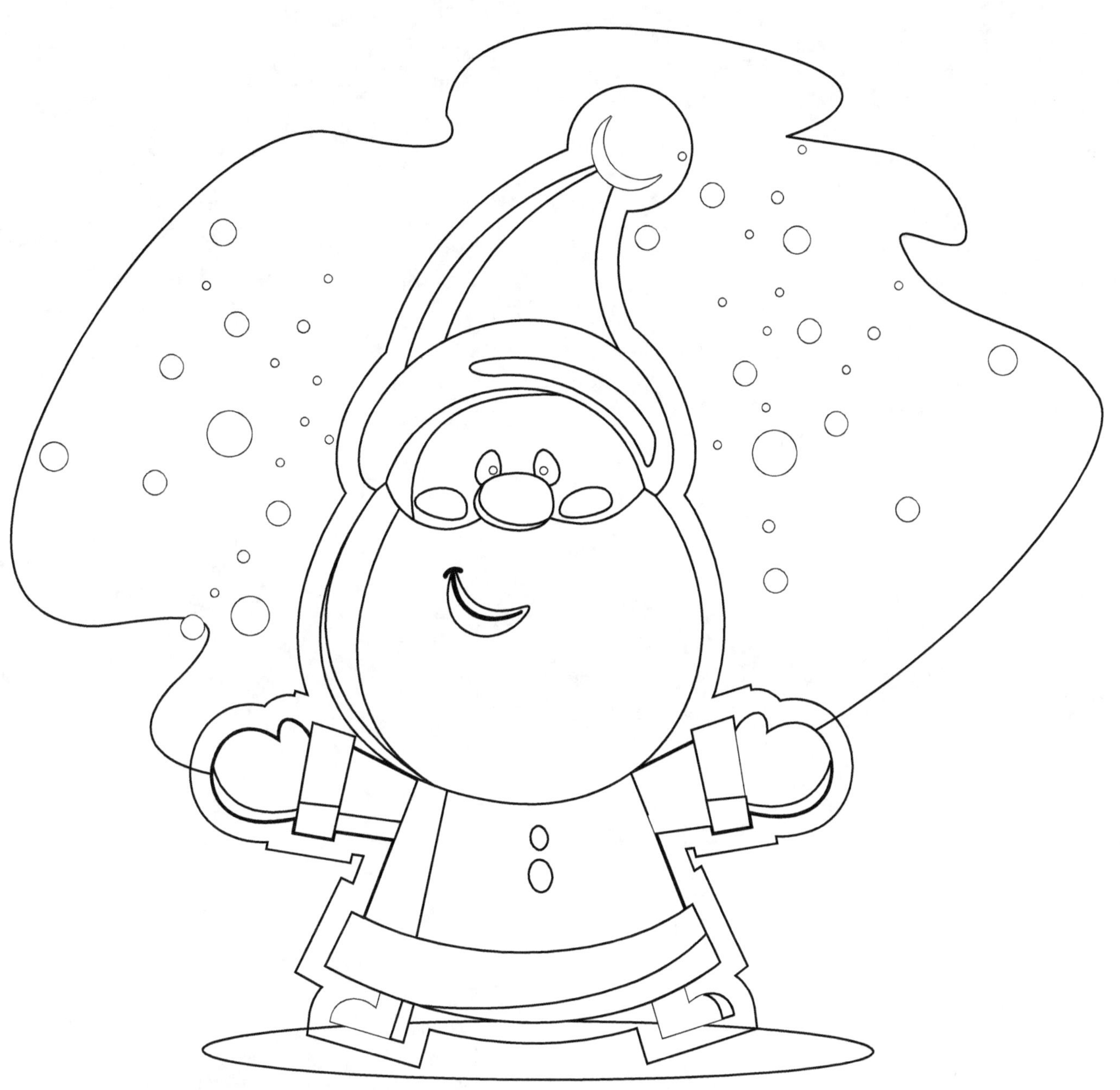

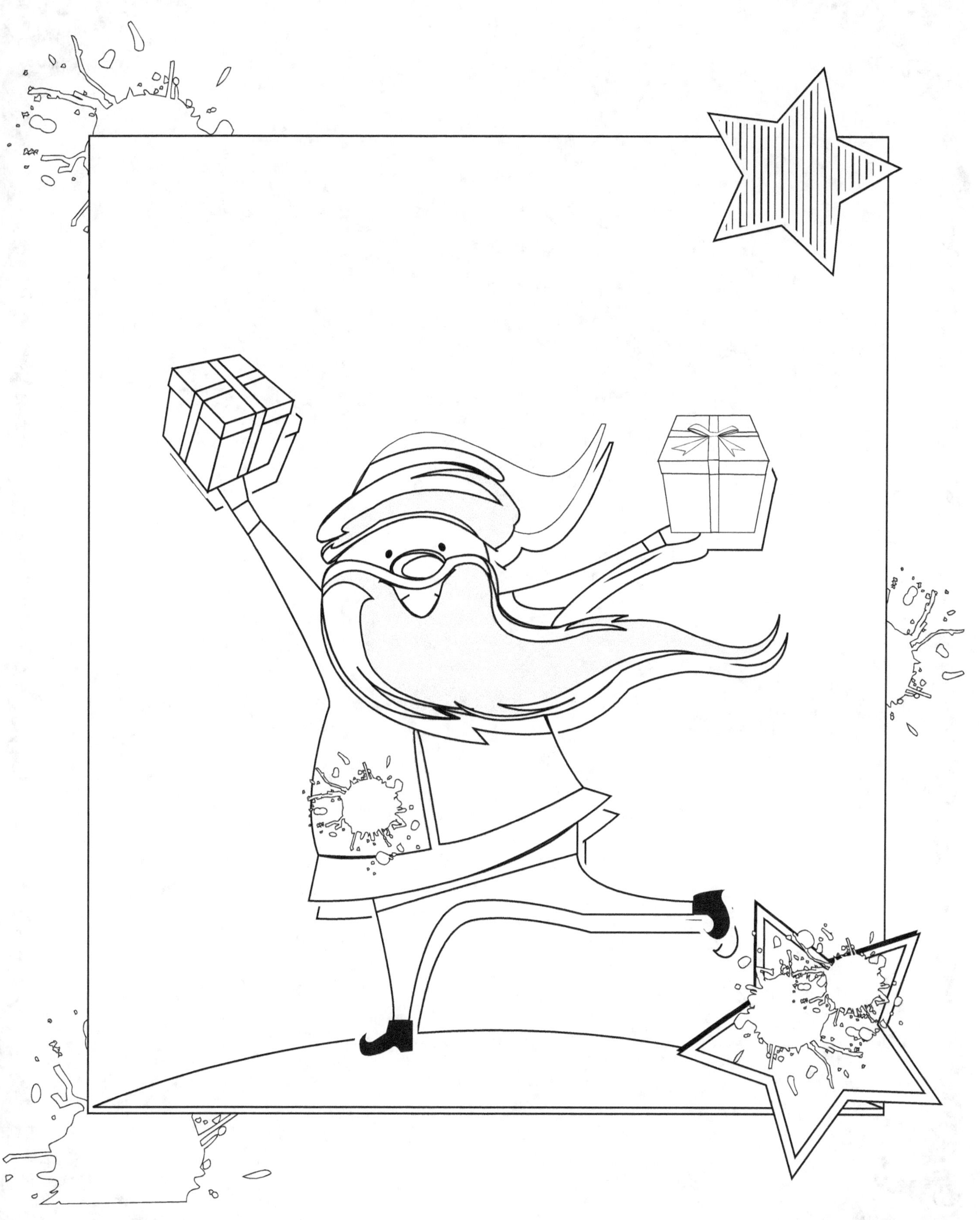

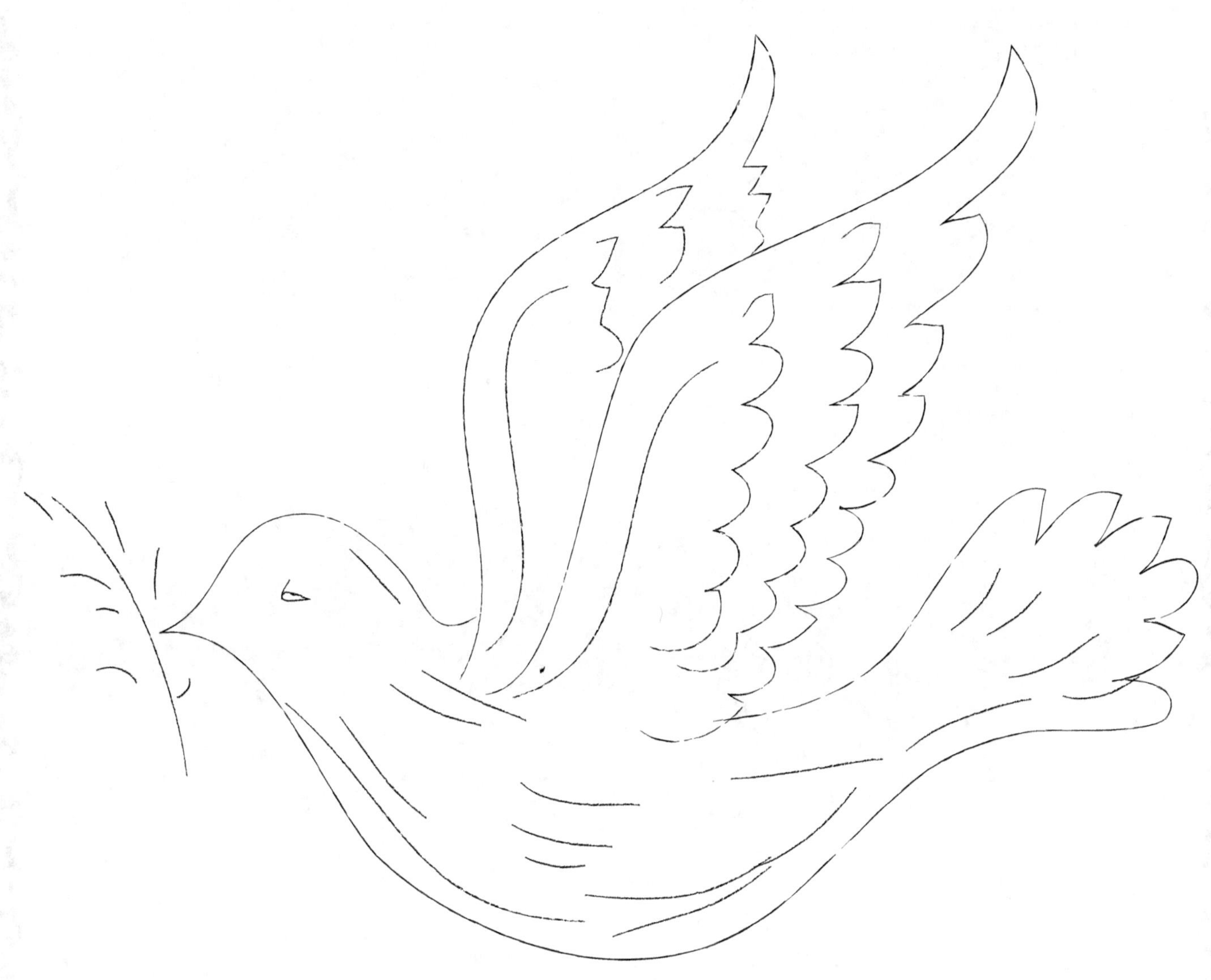

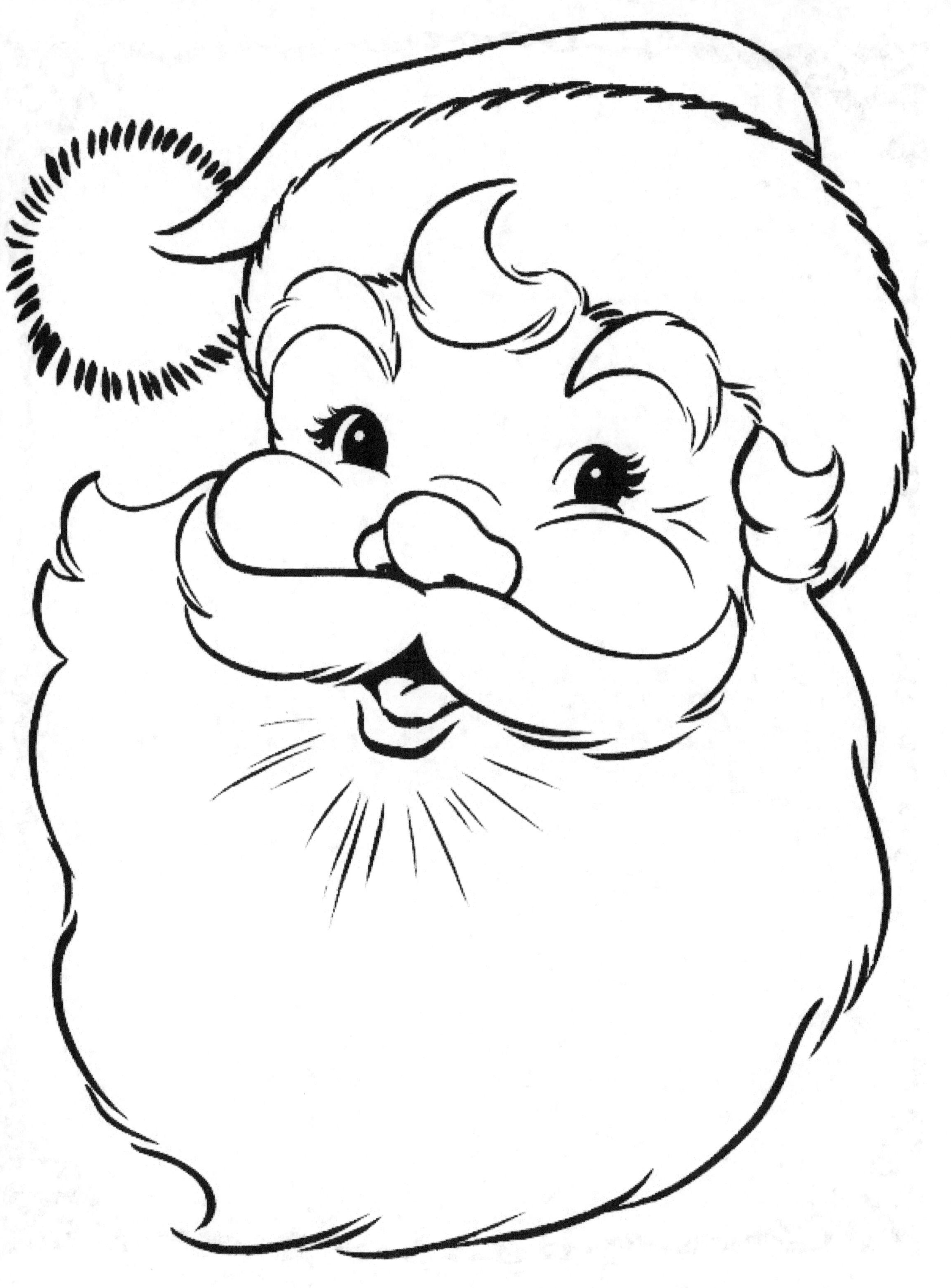

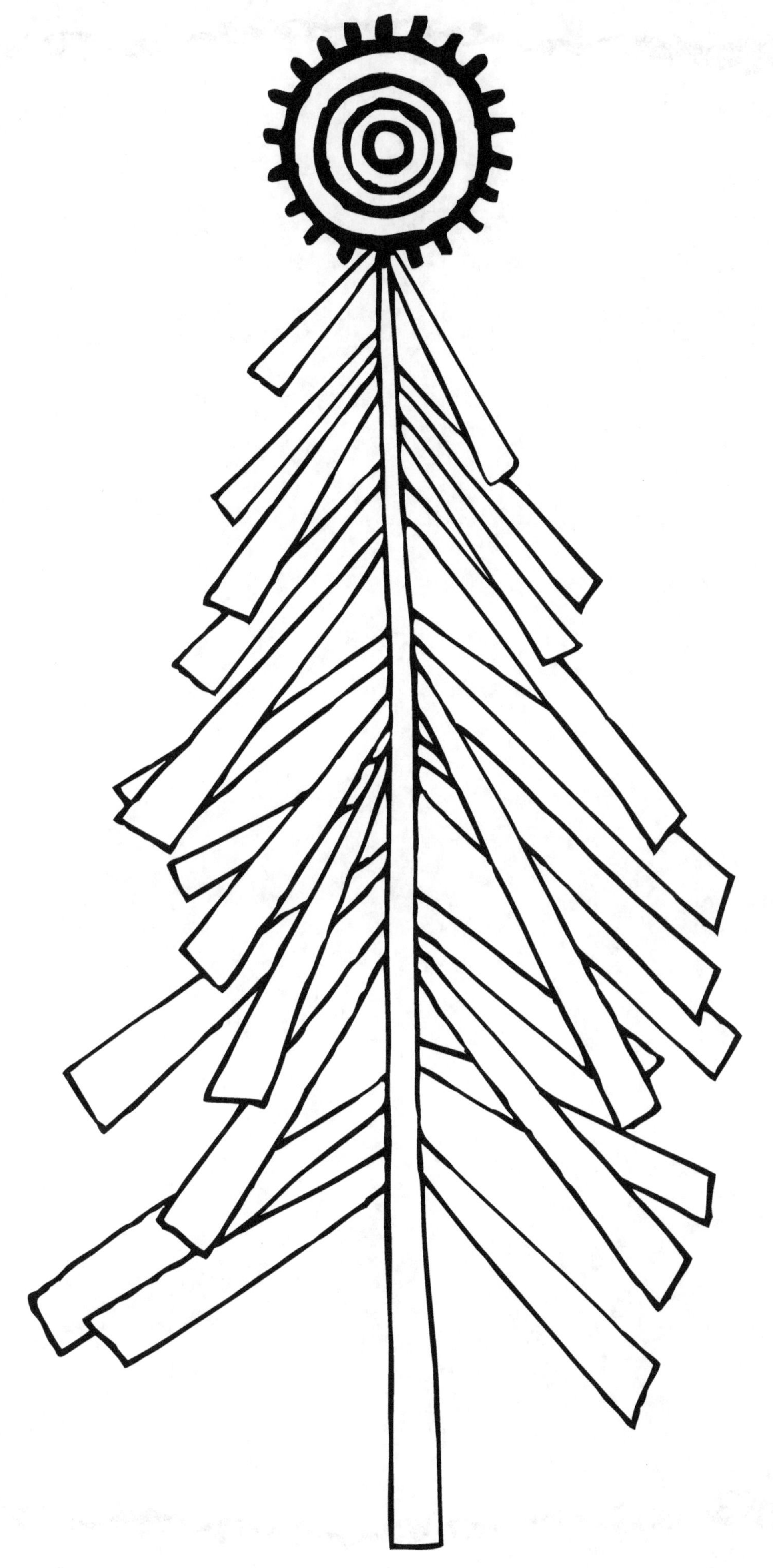

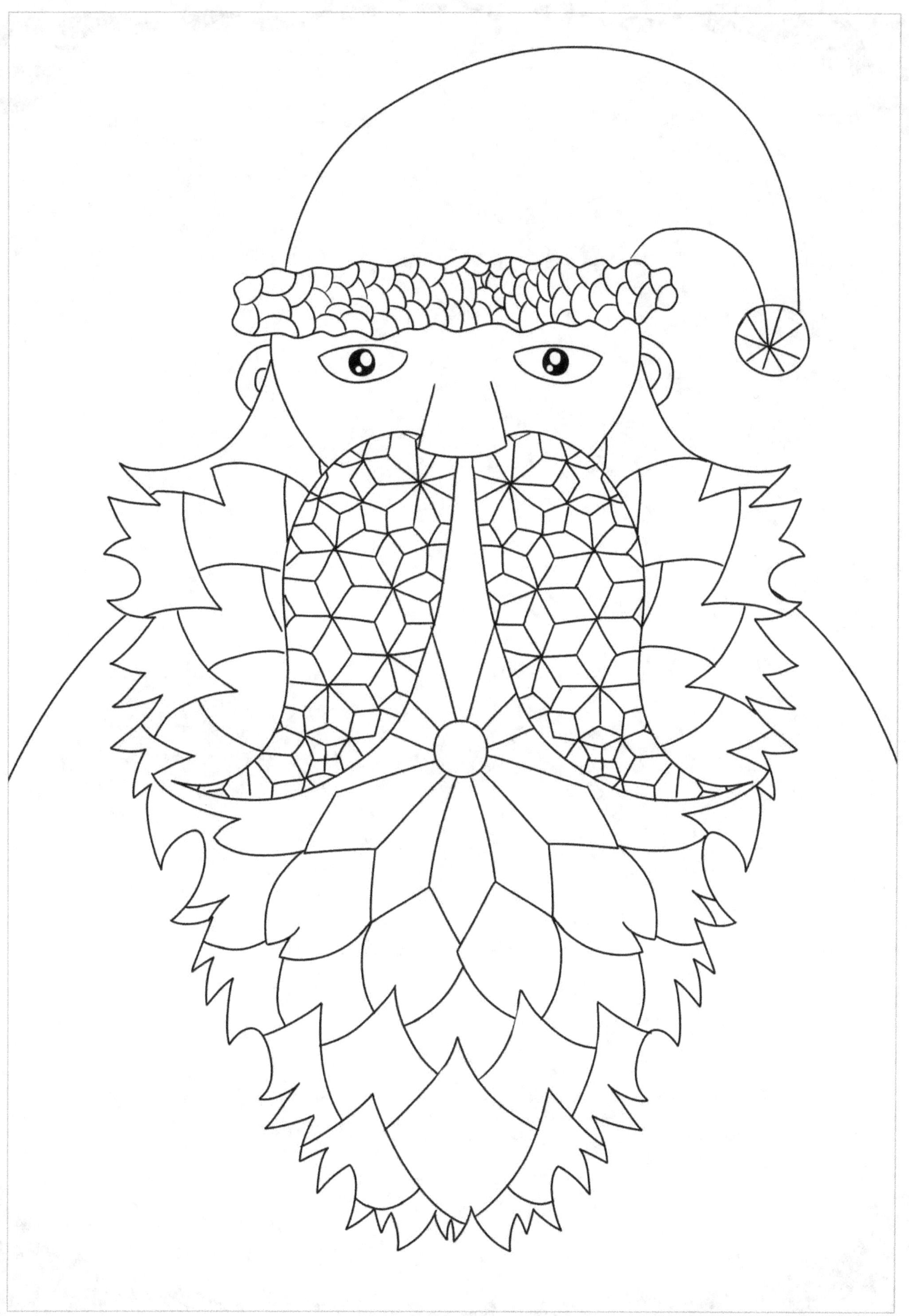

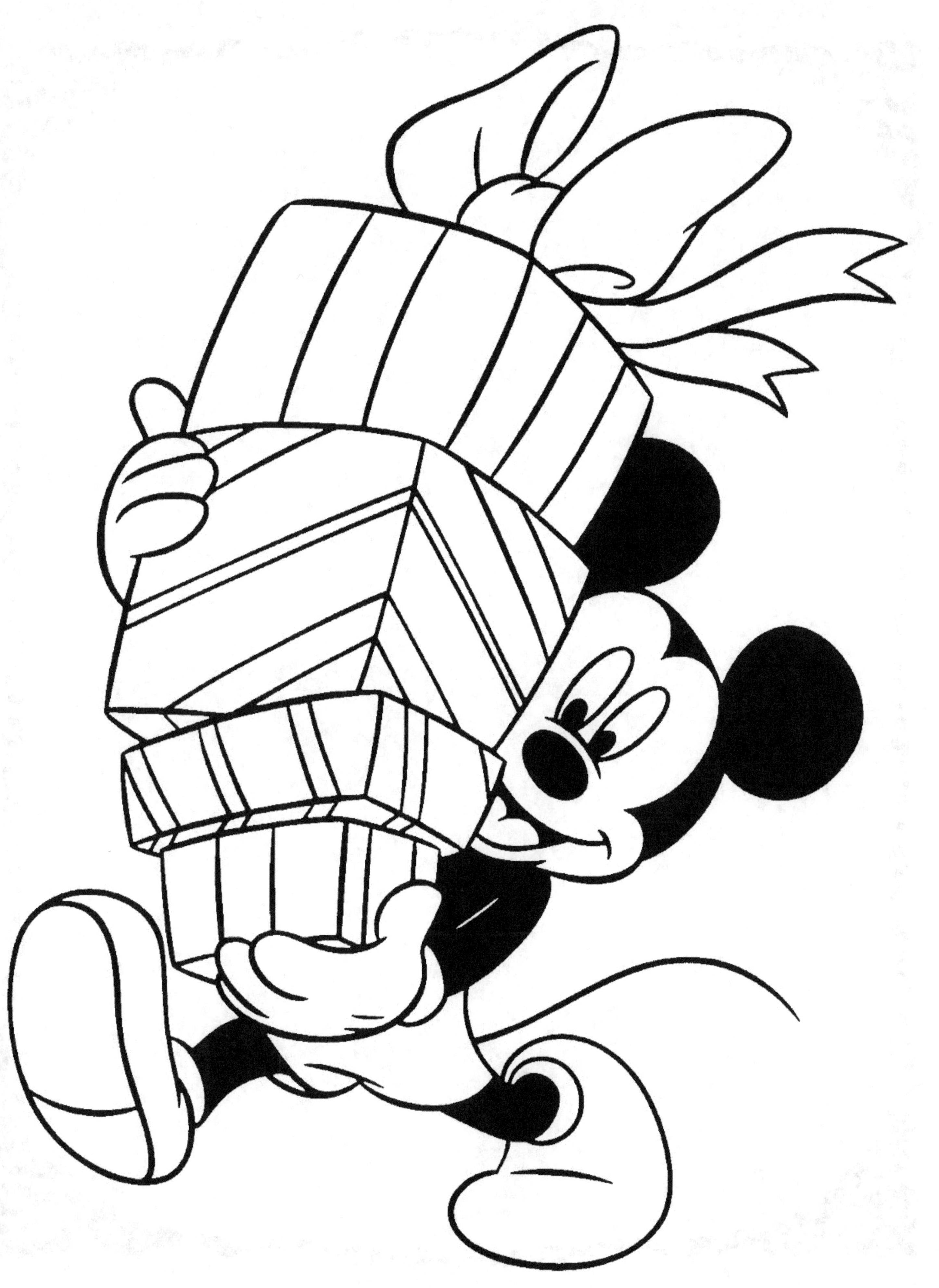

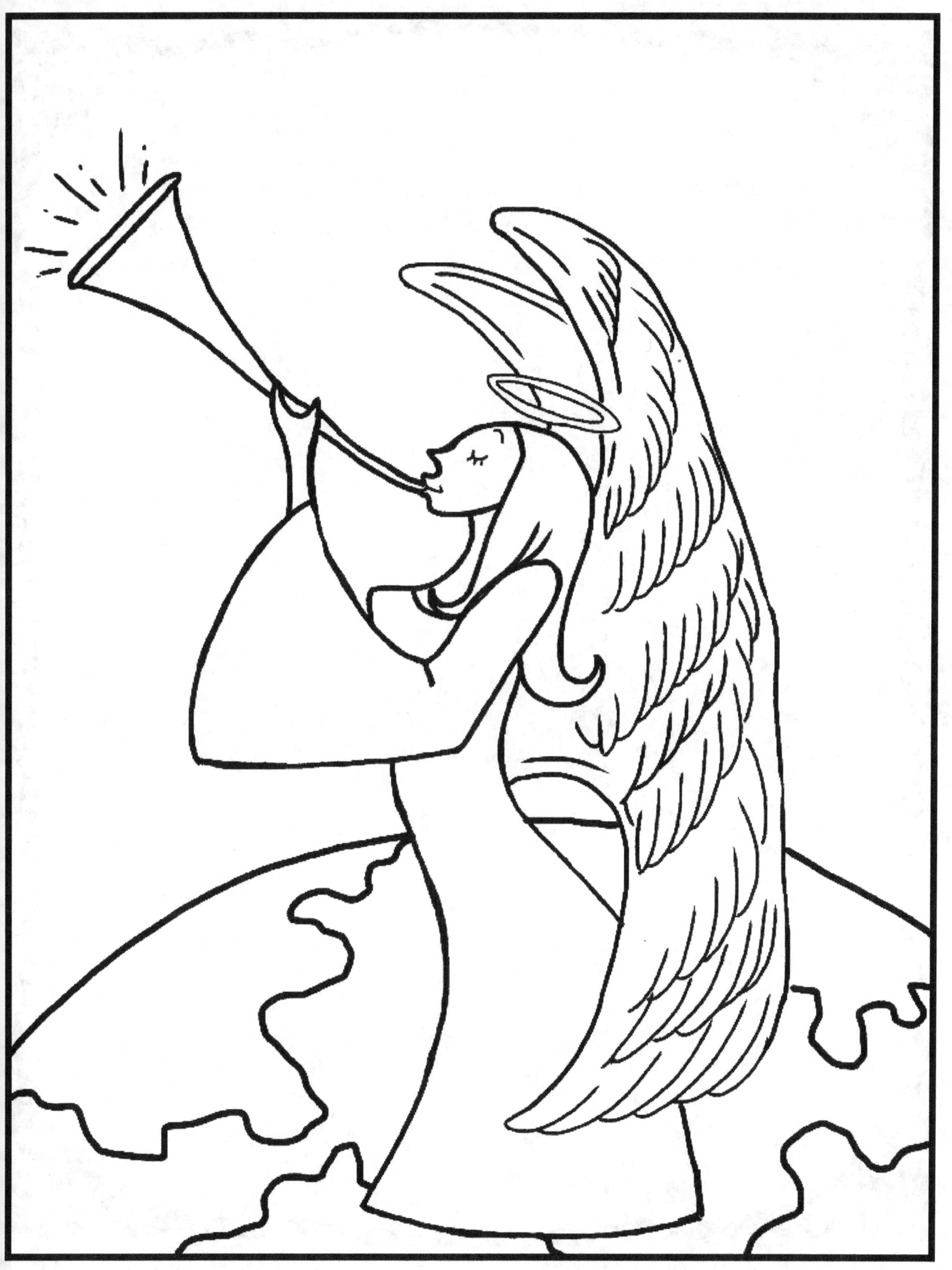

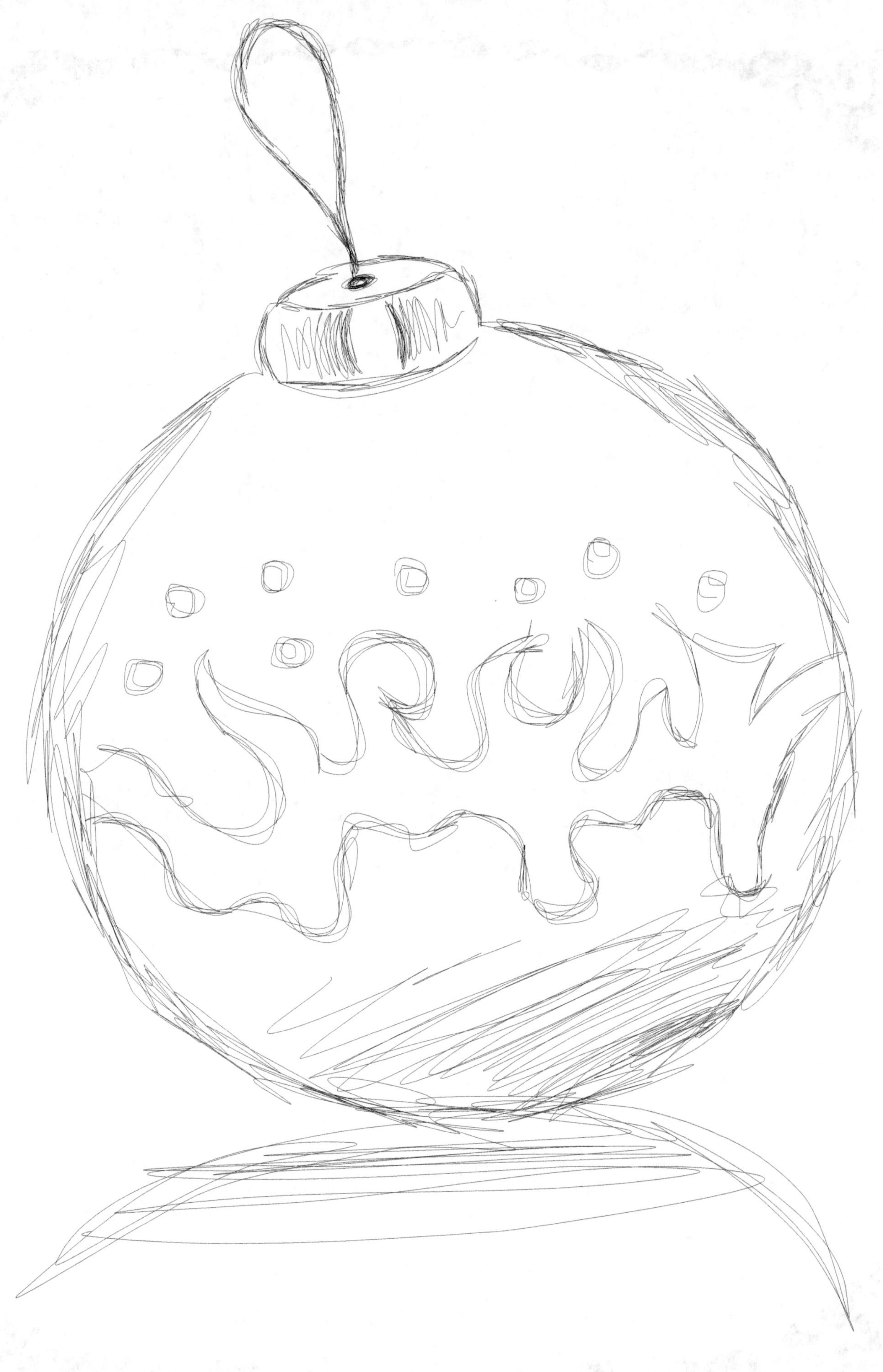

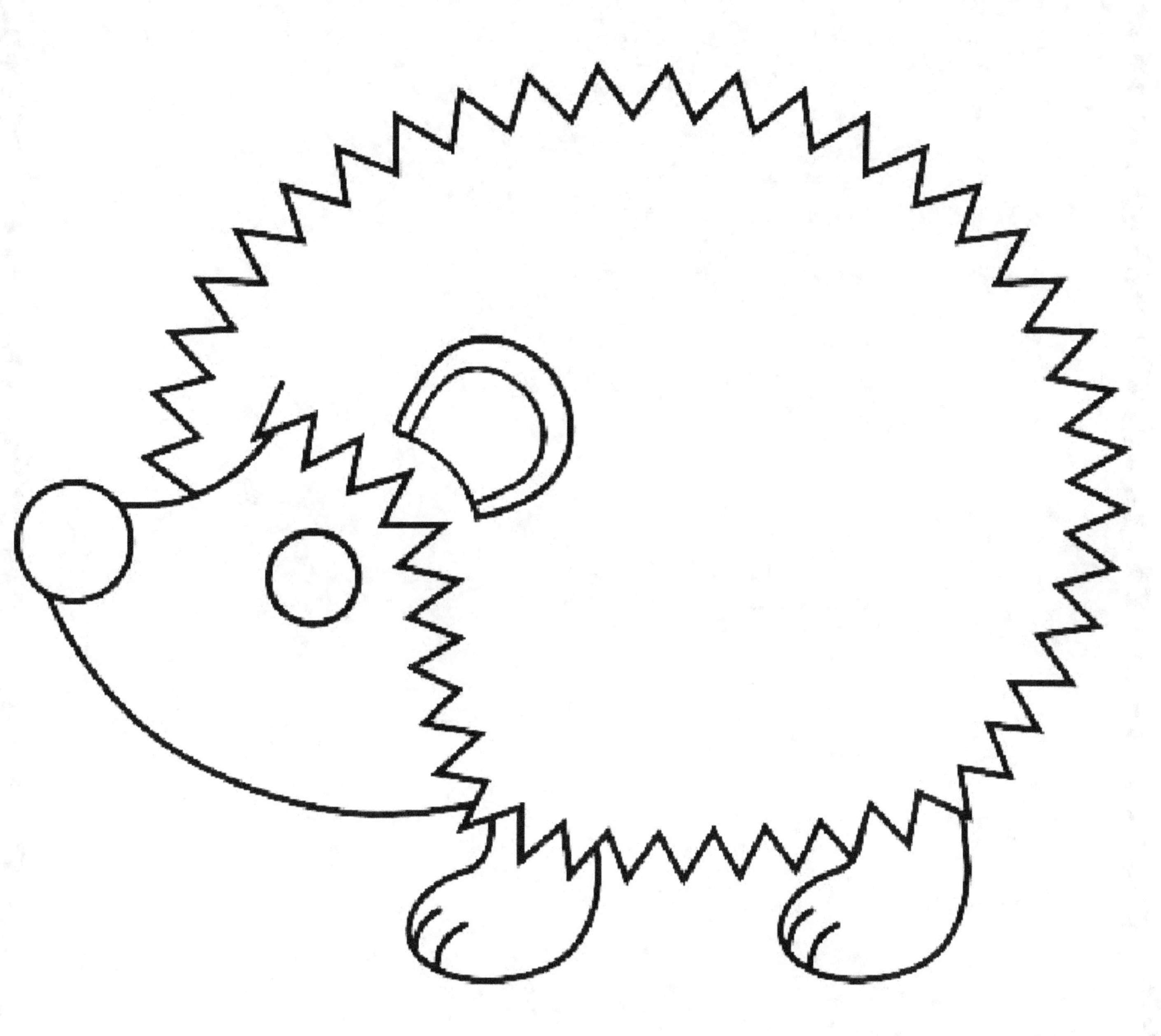

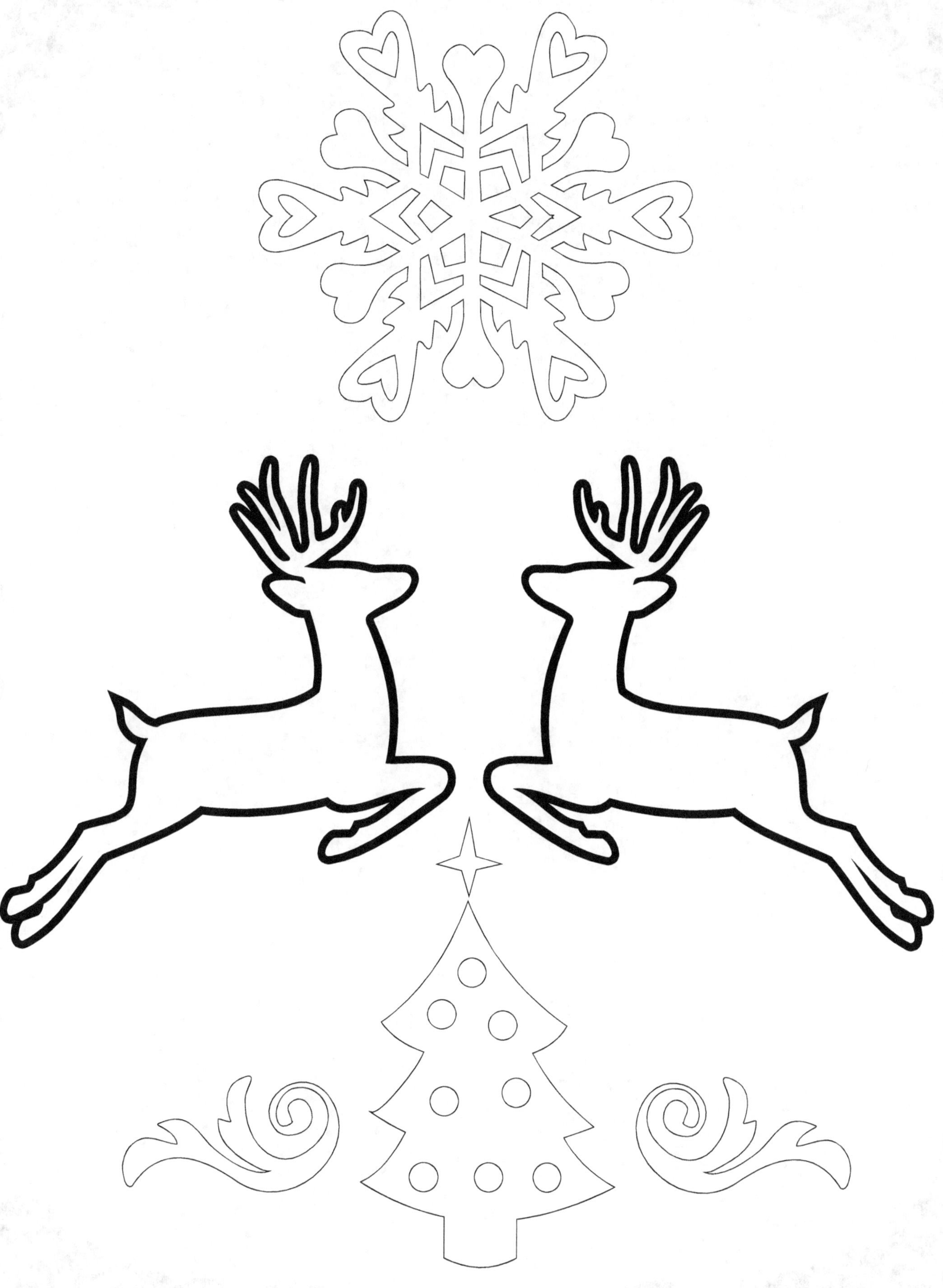

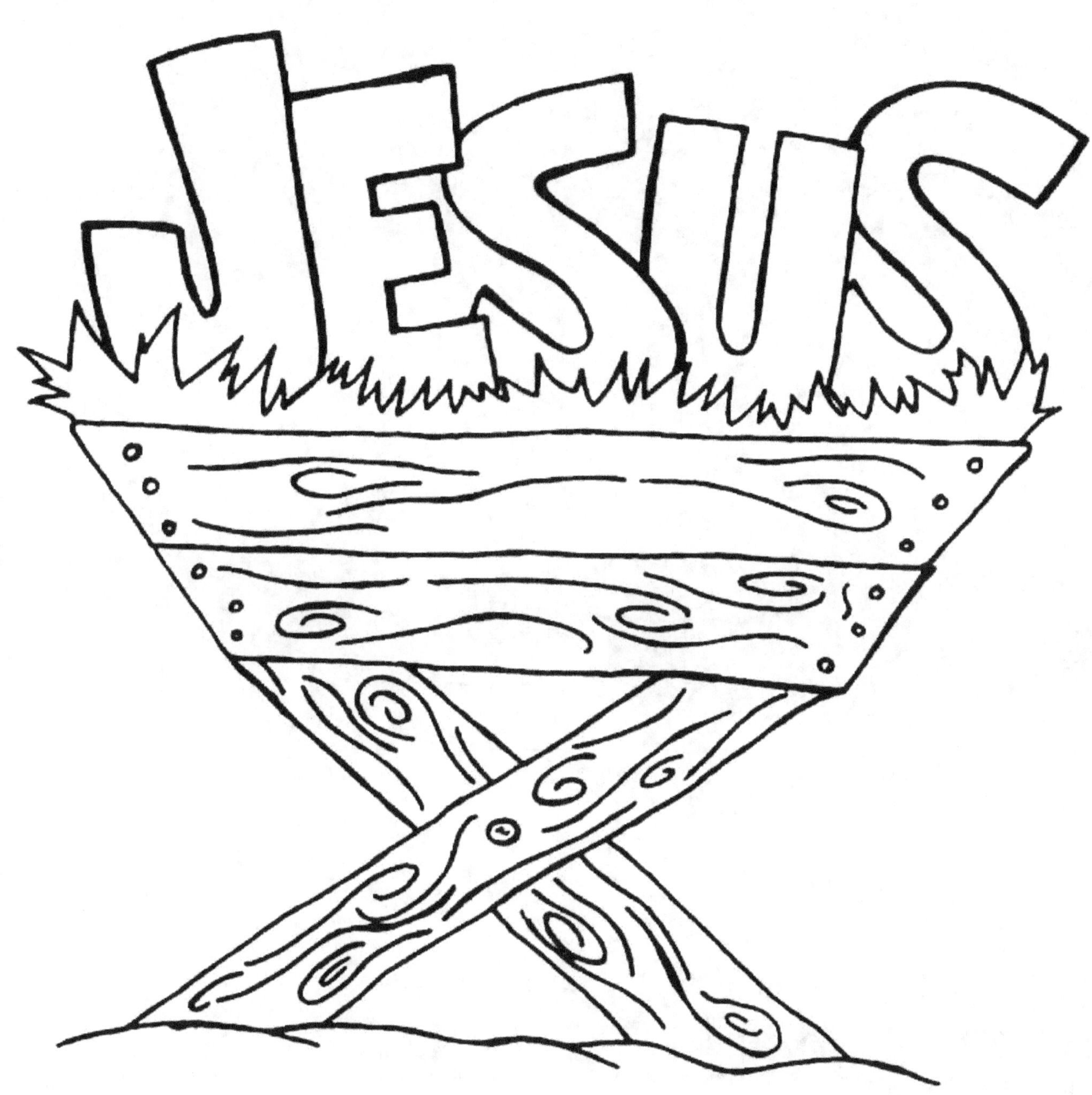

JESUS

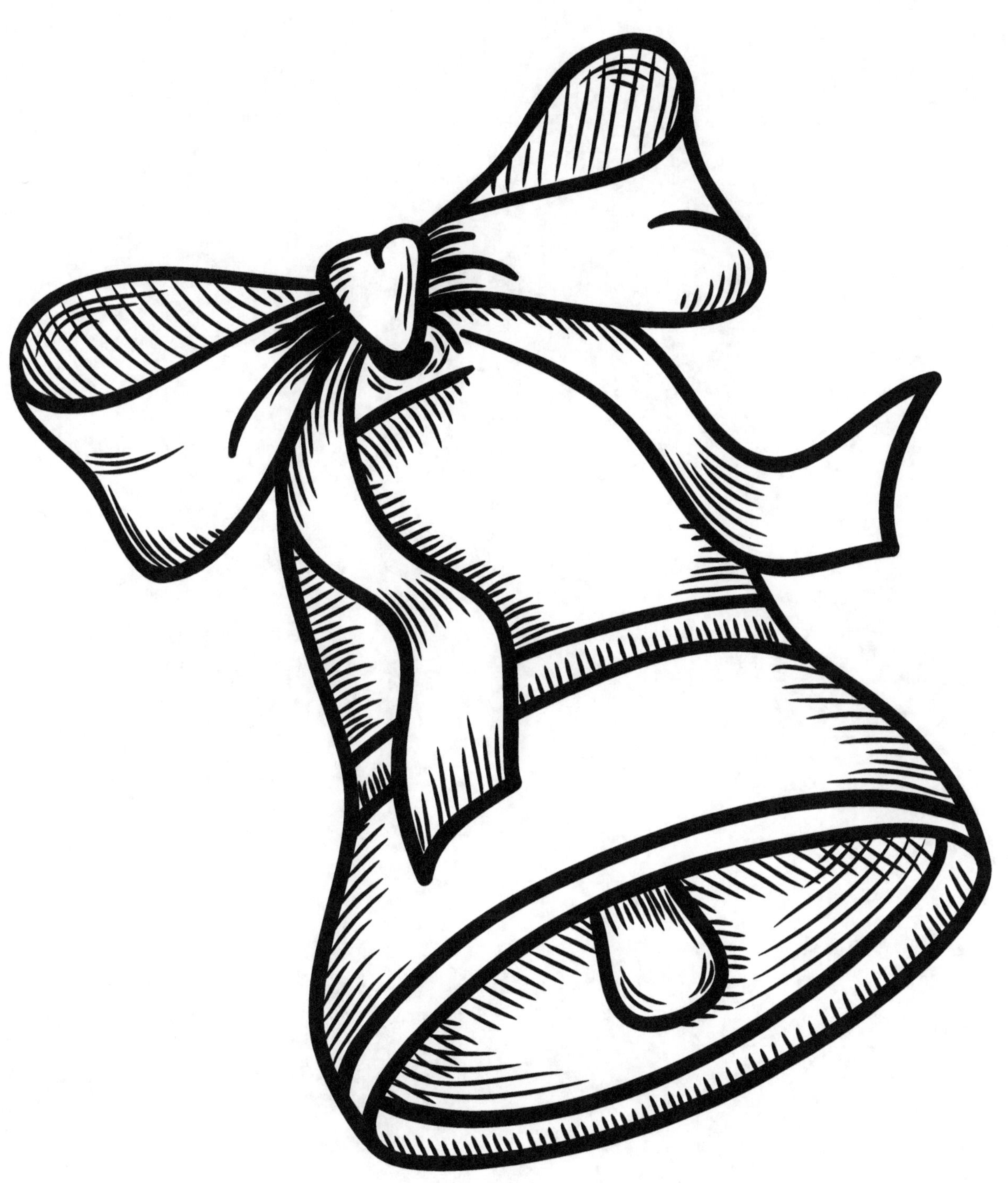

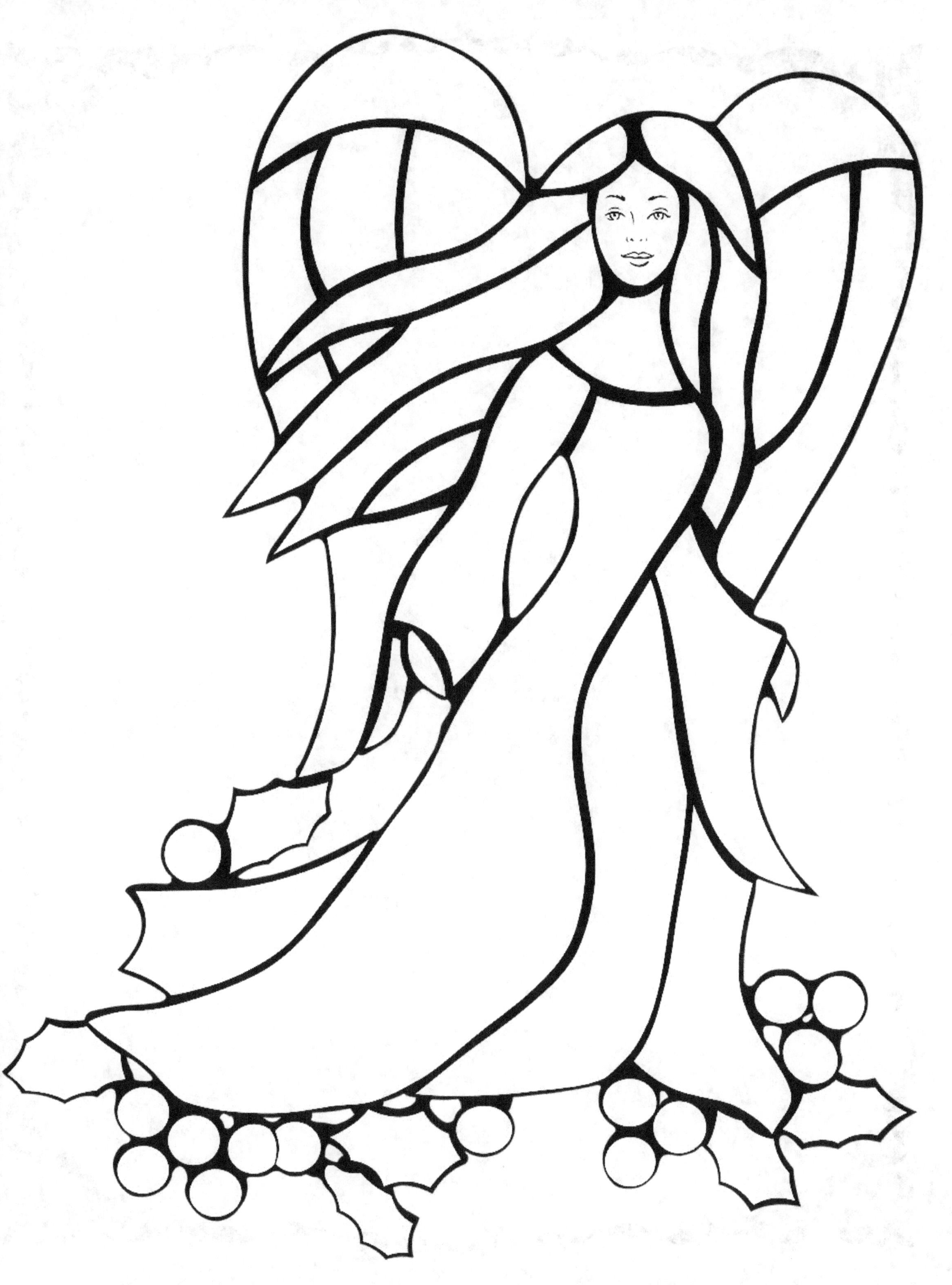

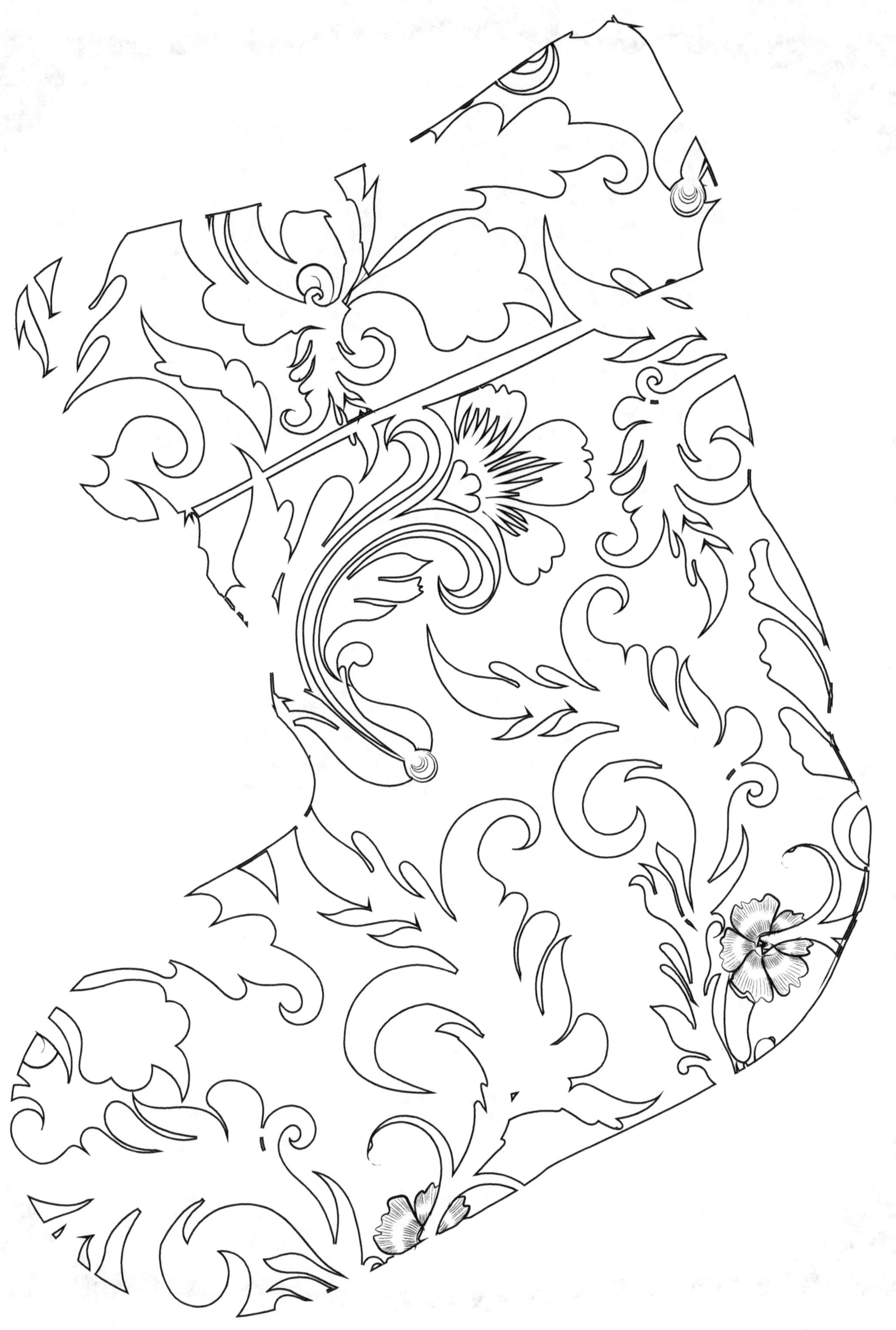

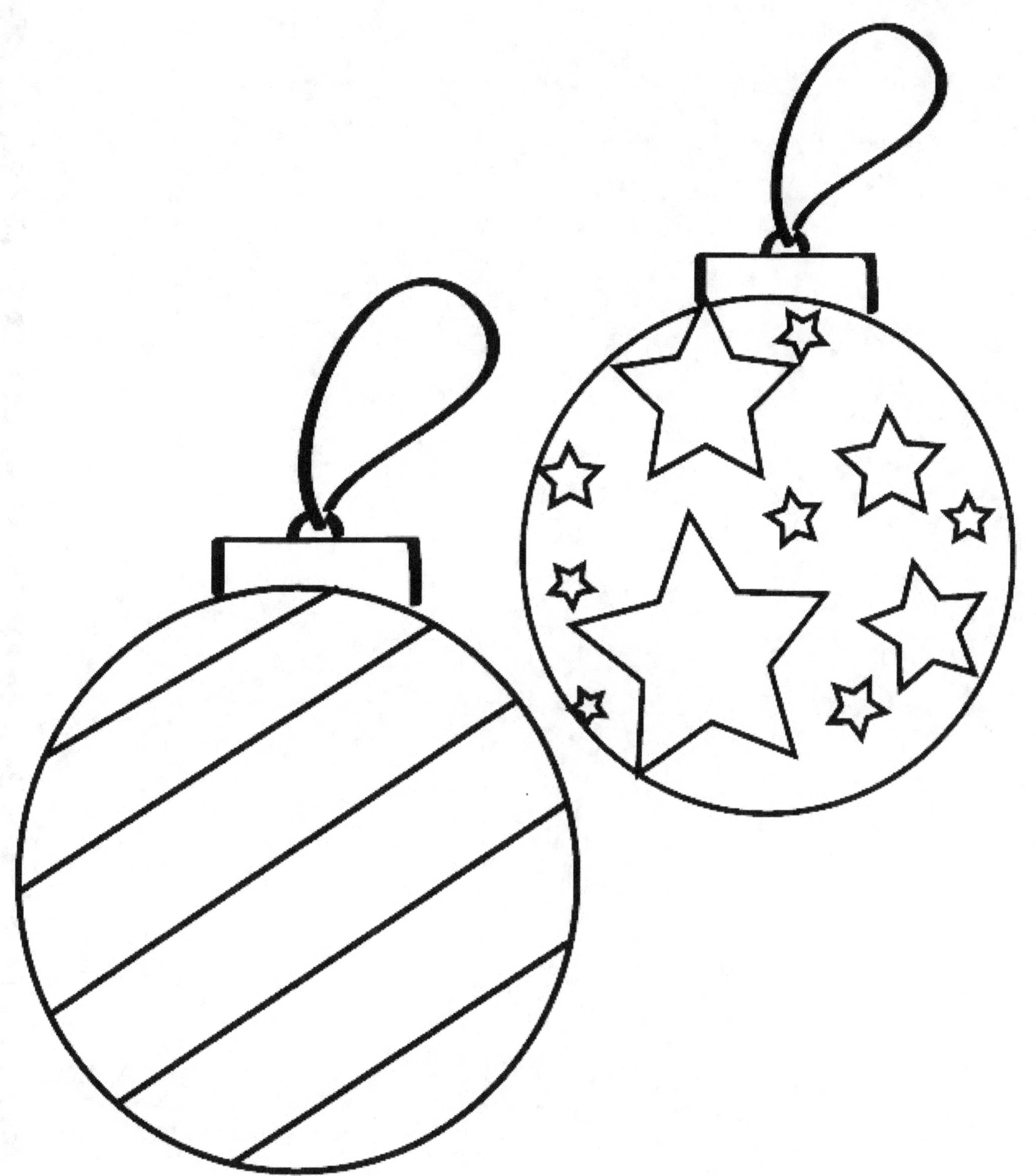

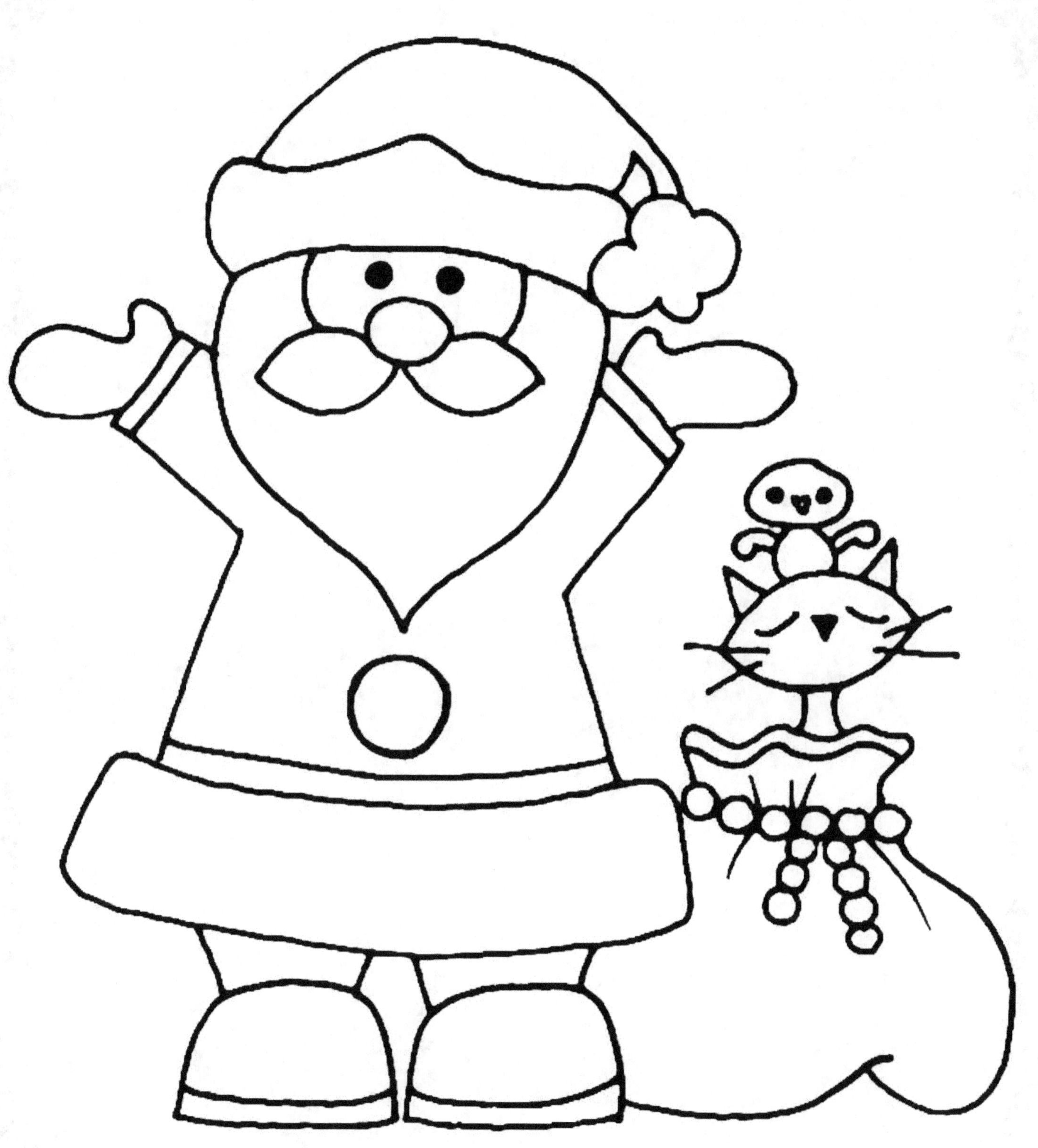

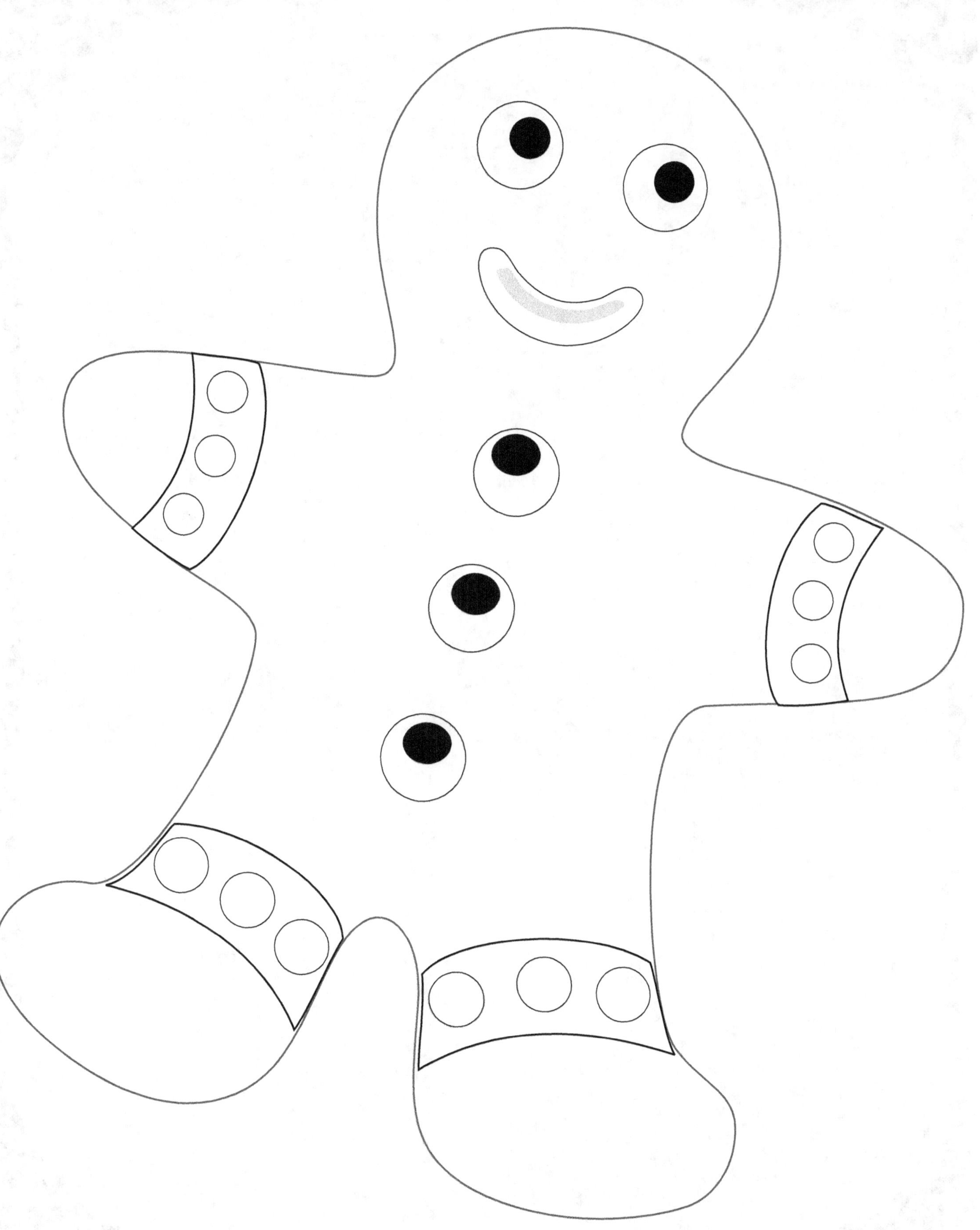

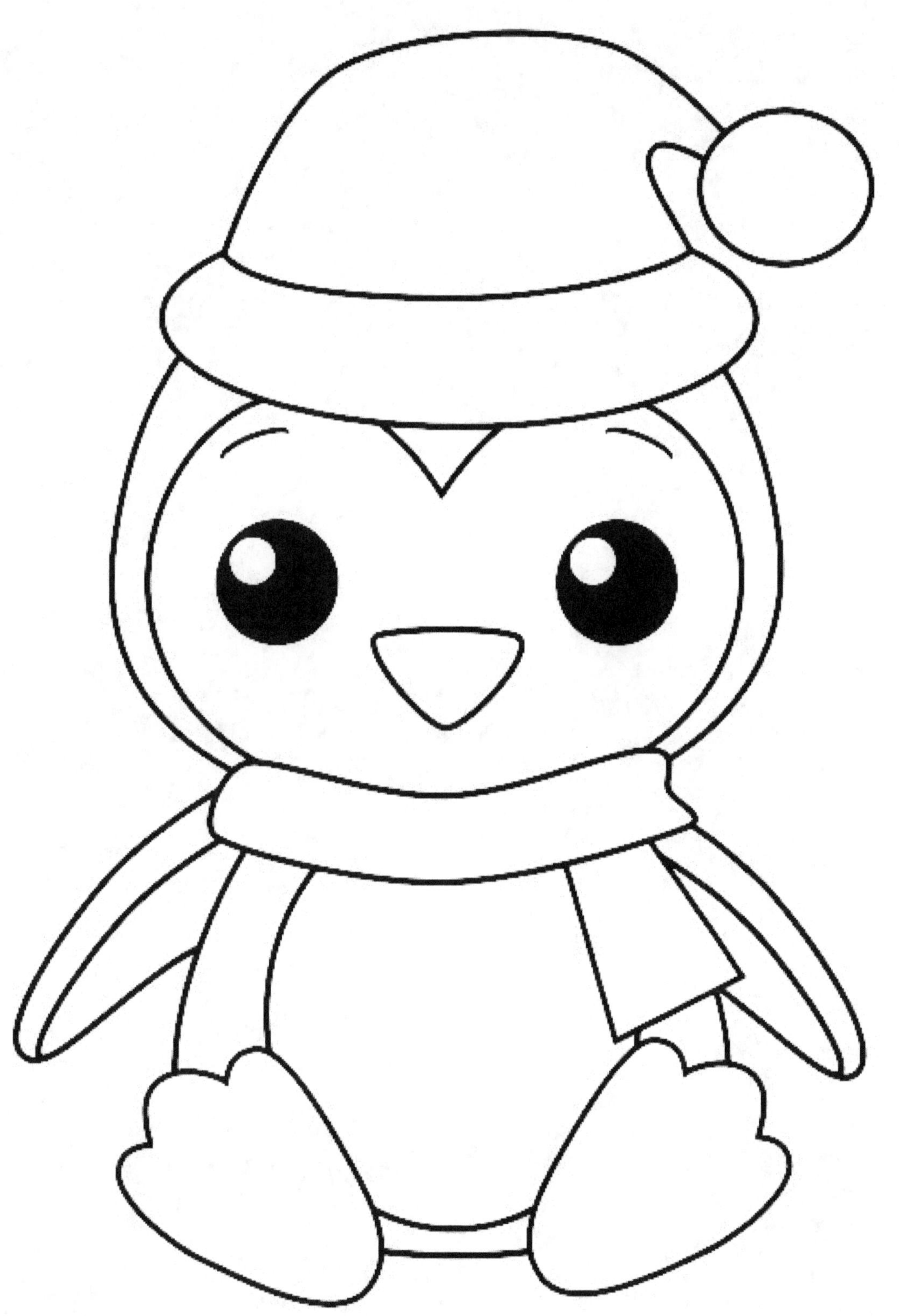

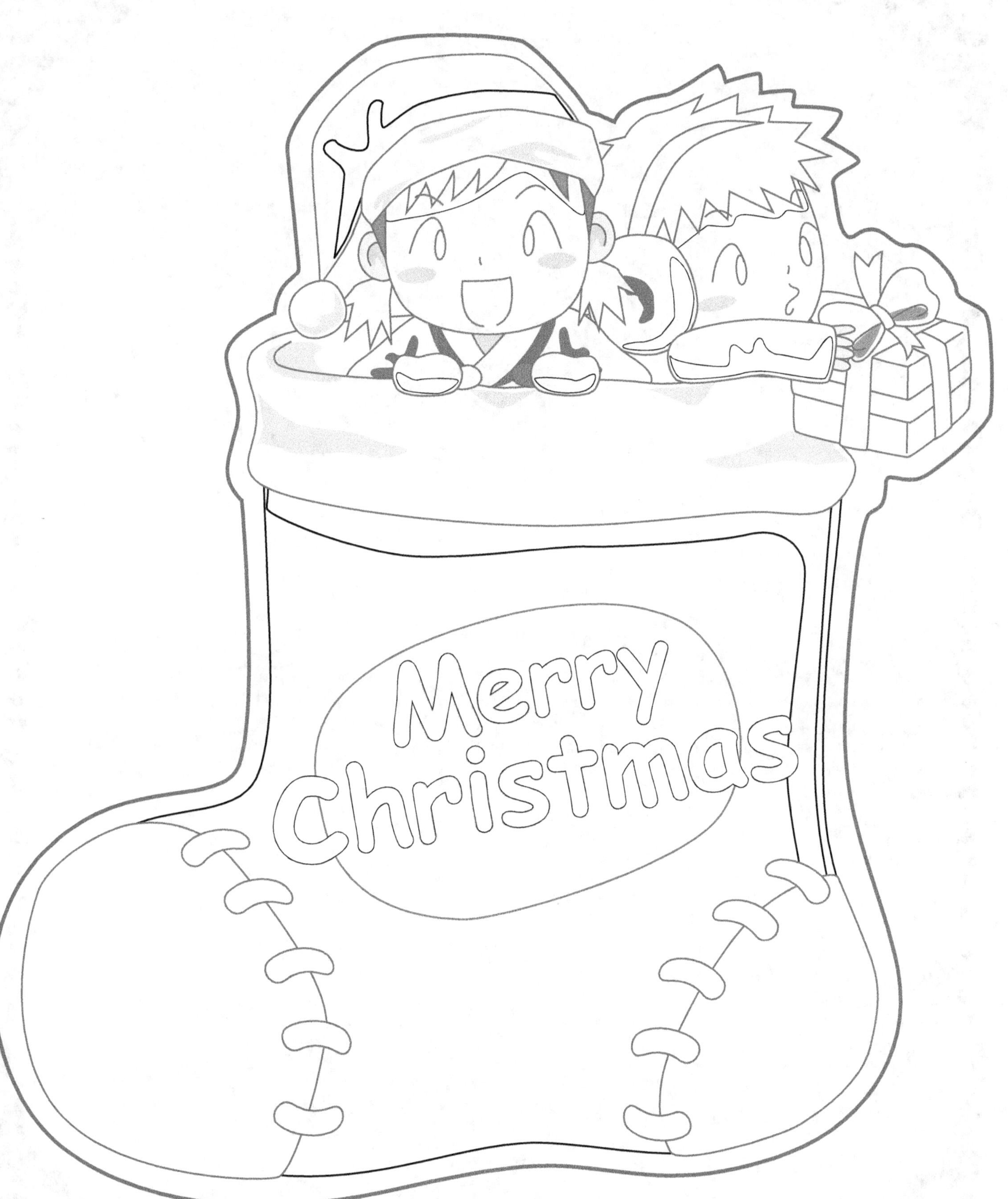
Merry
Christmas

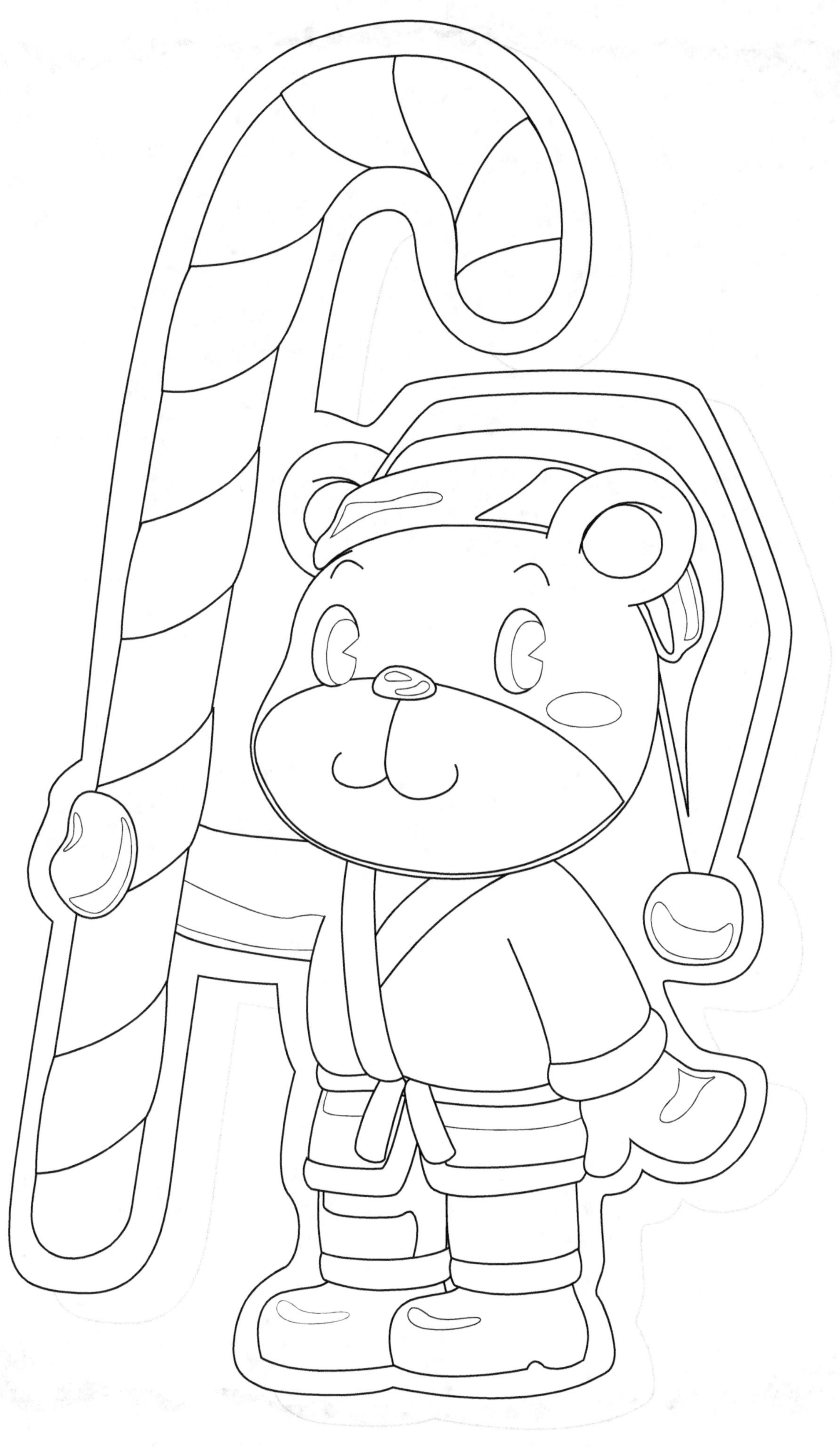

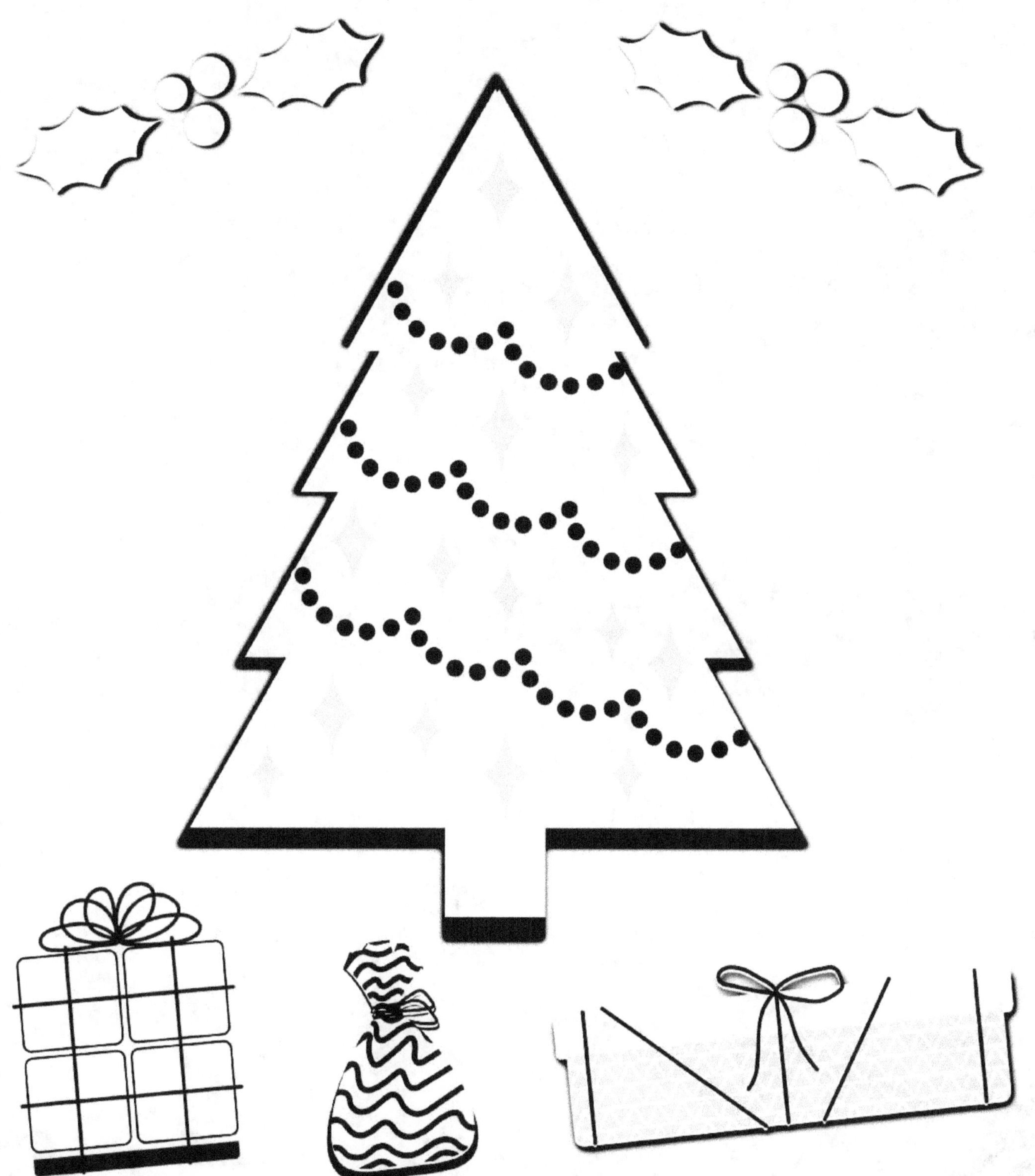

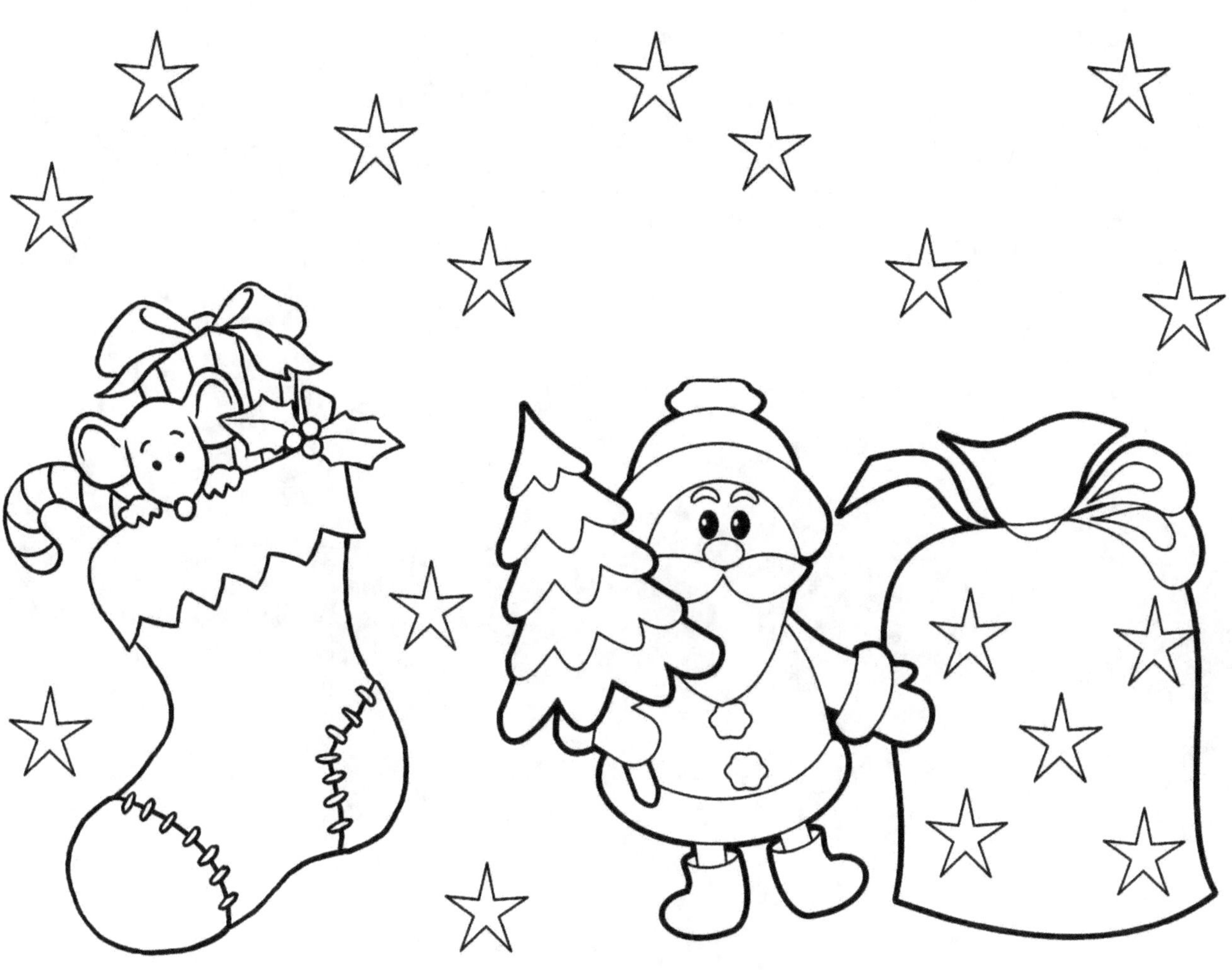

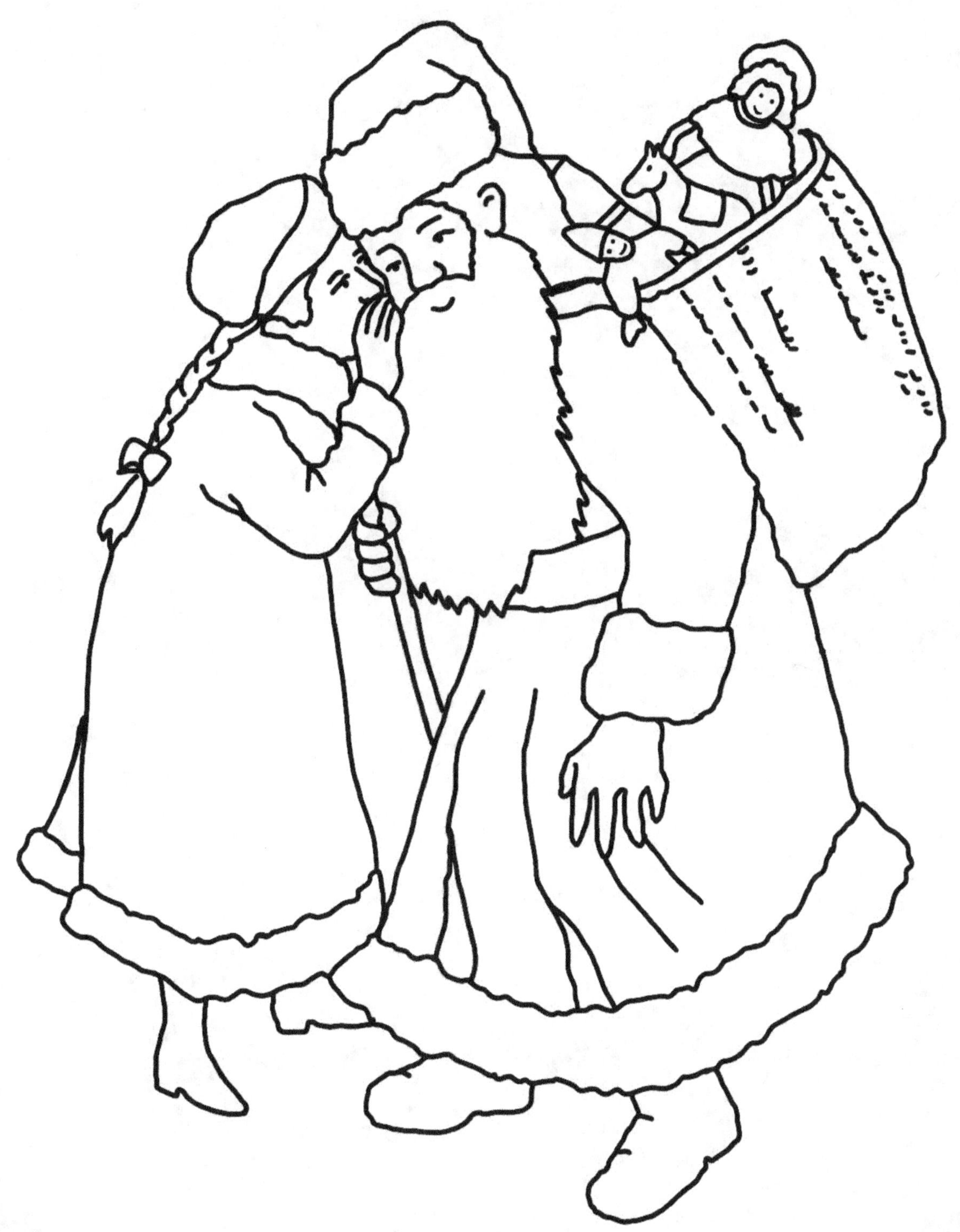

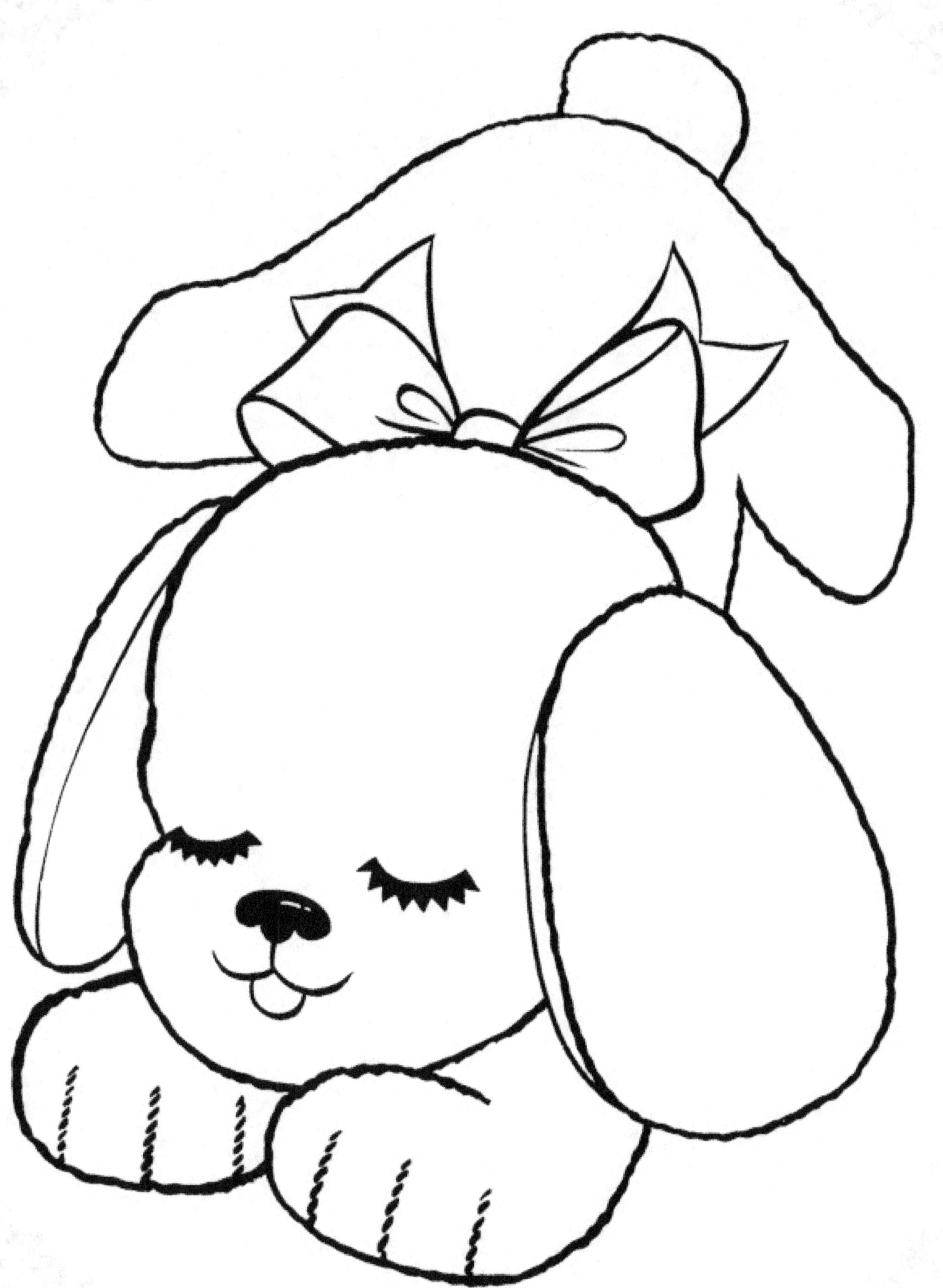

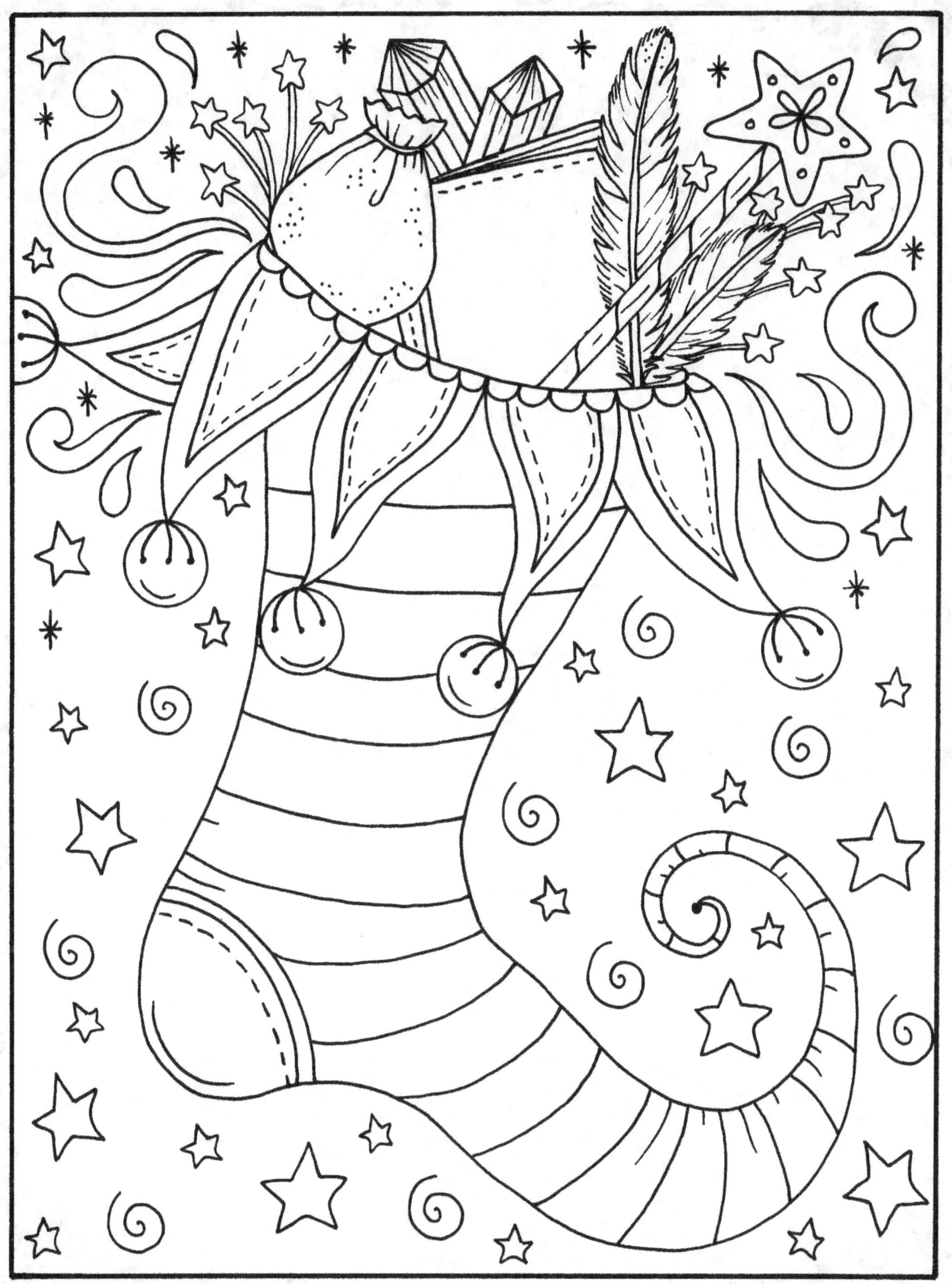

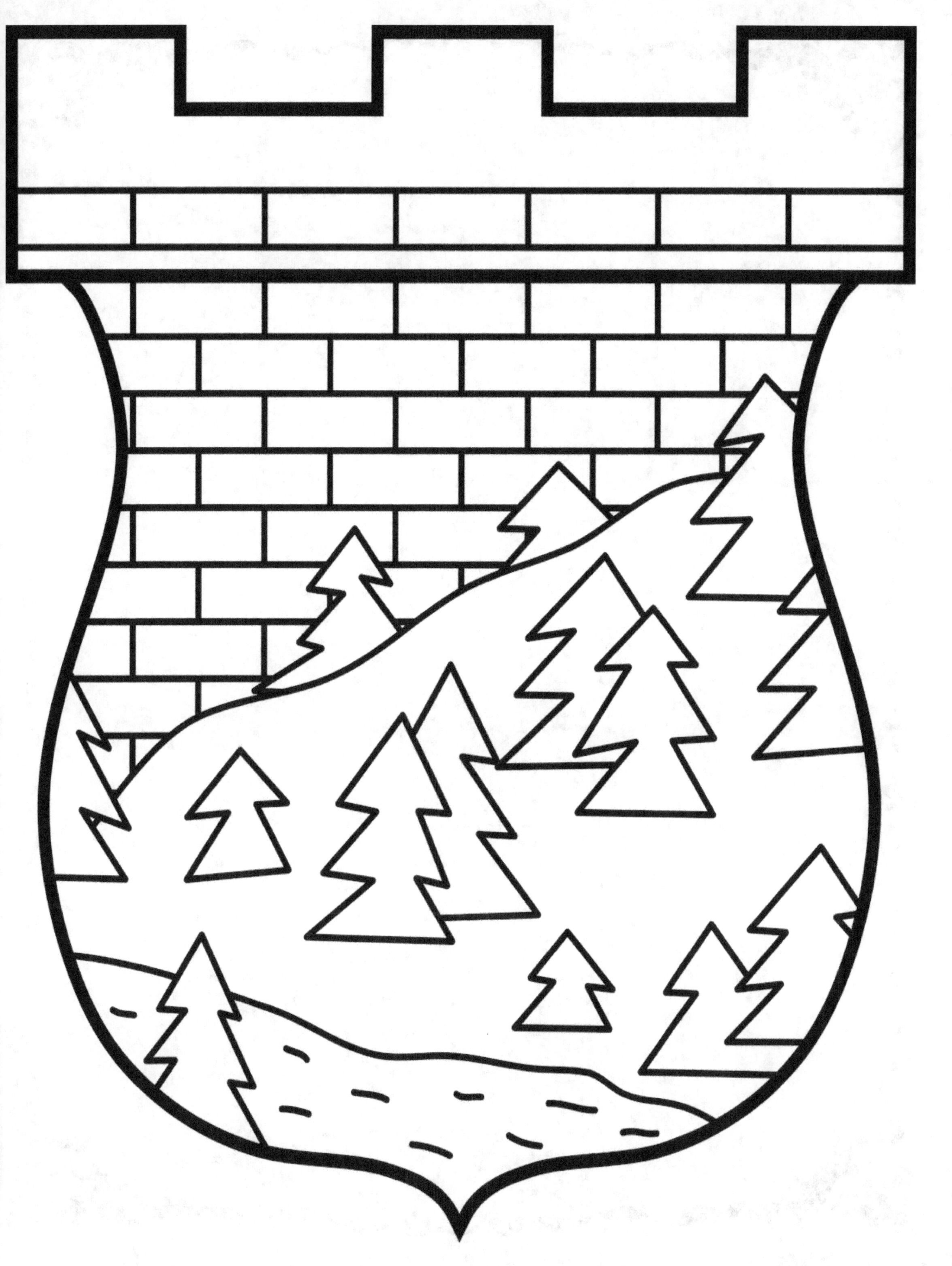

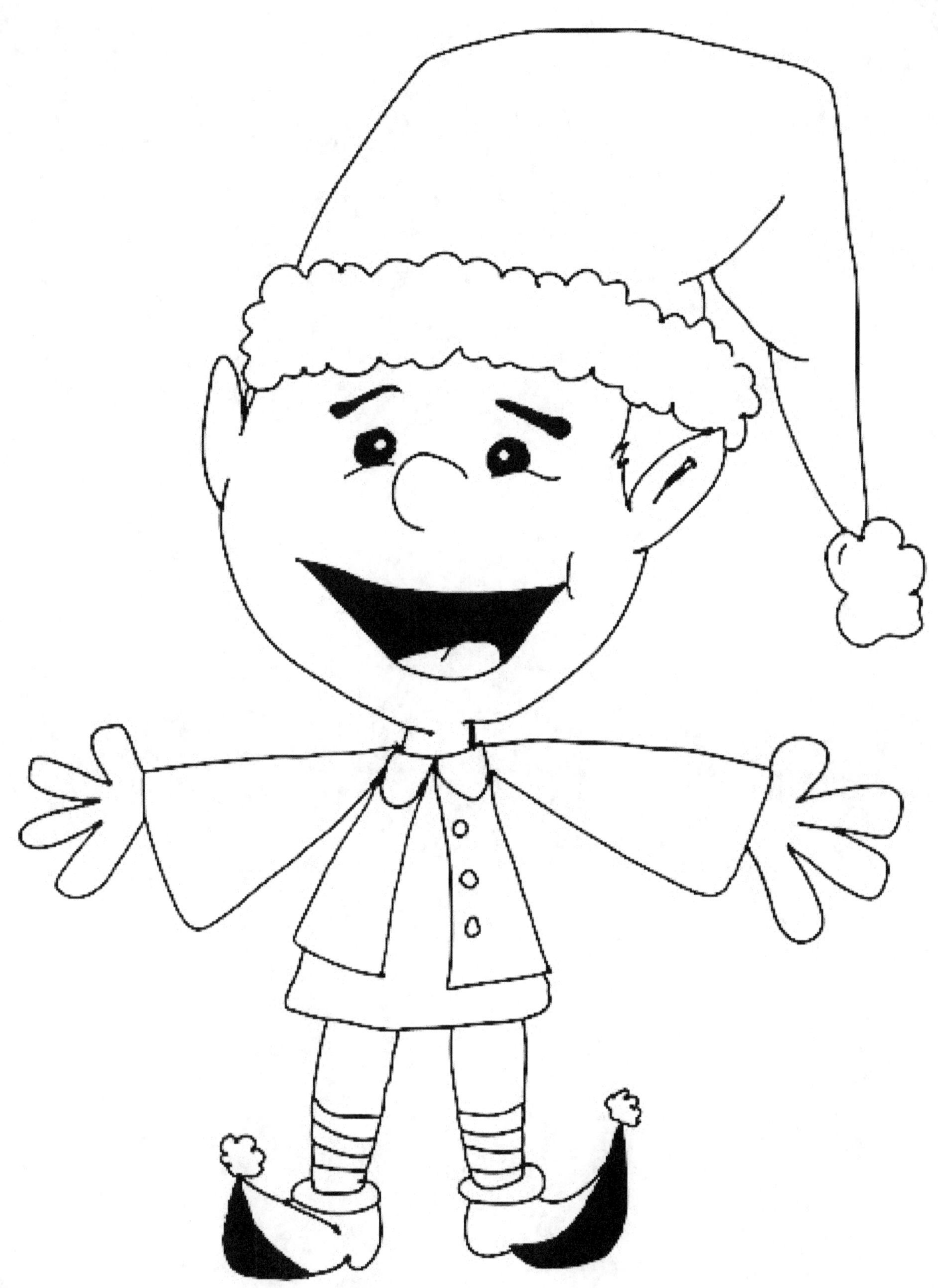

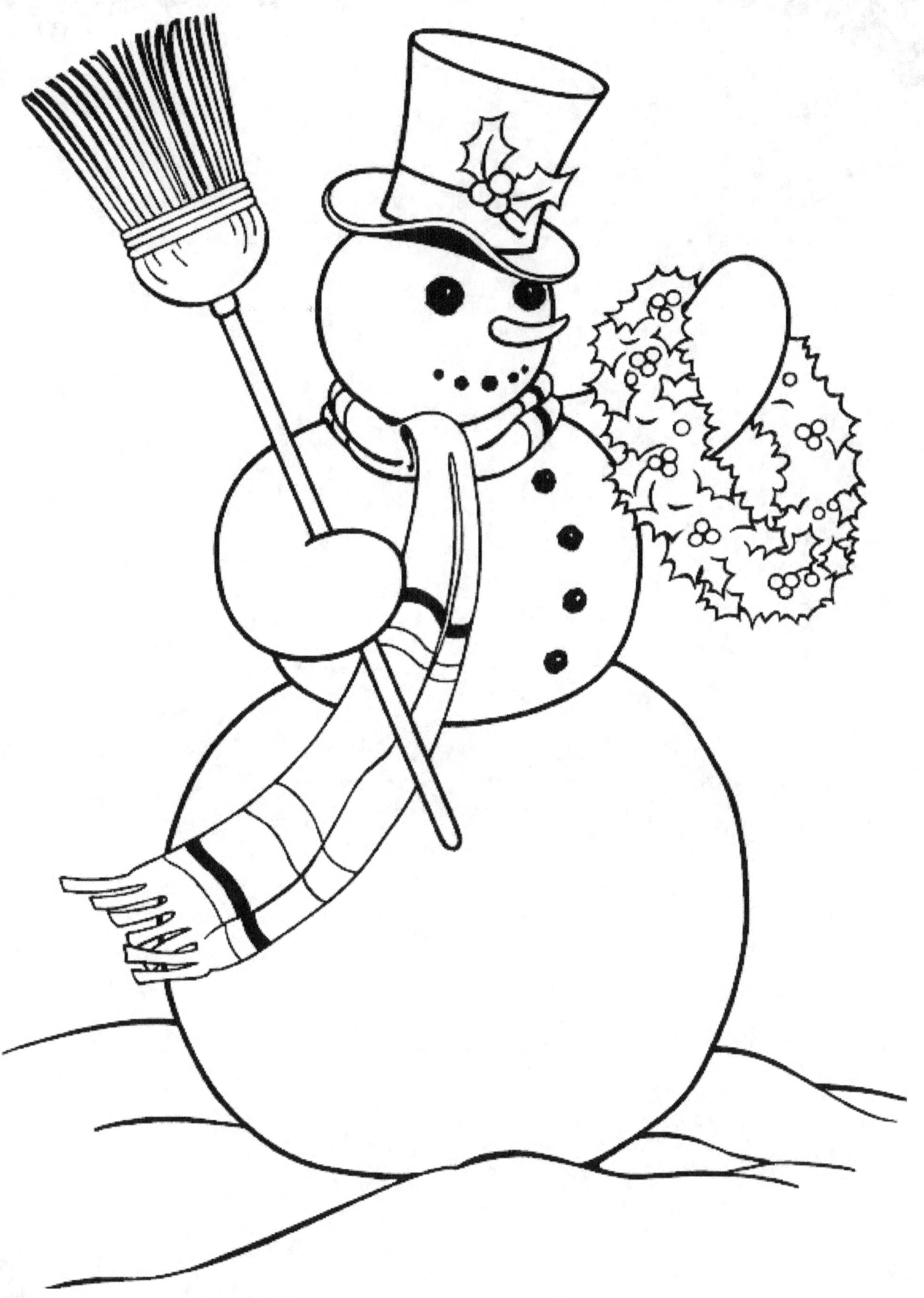

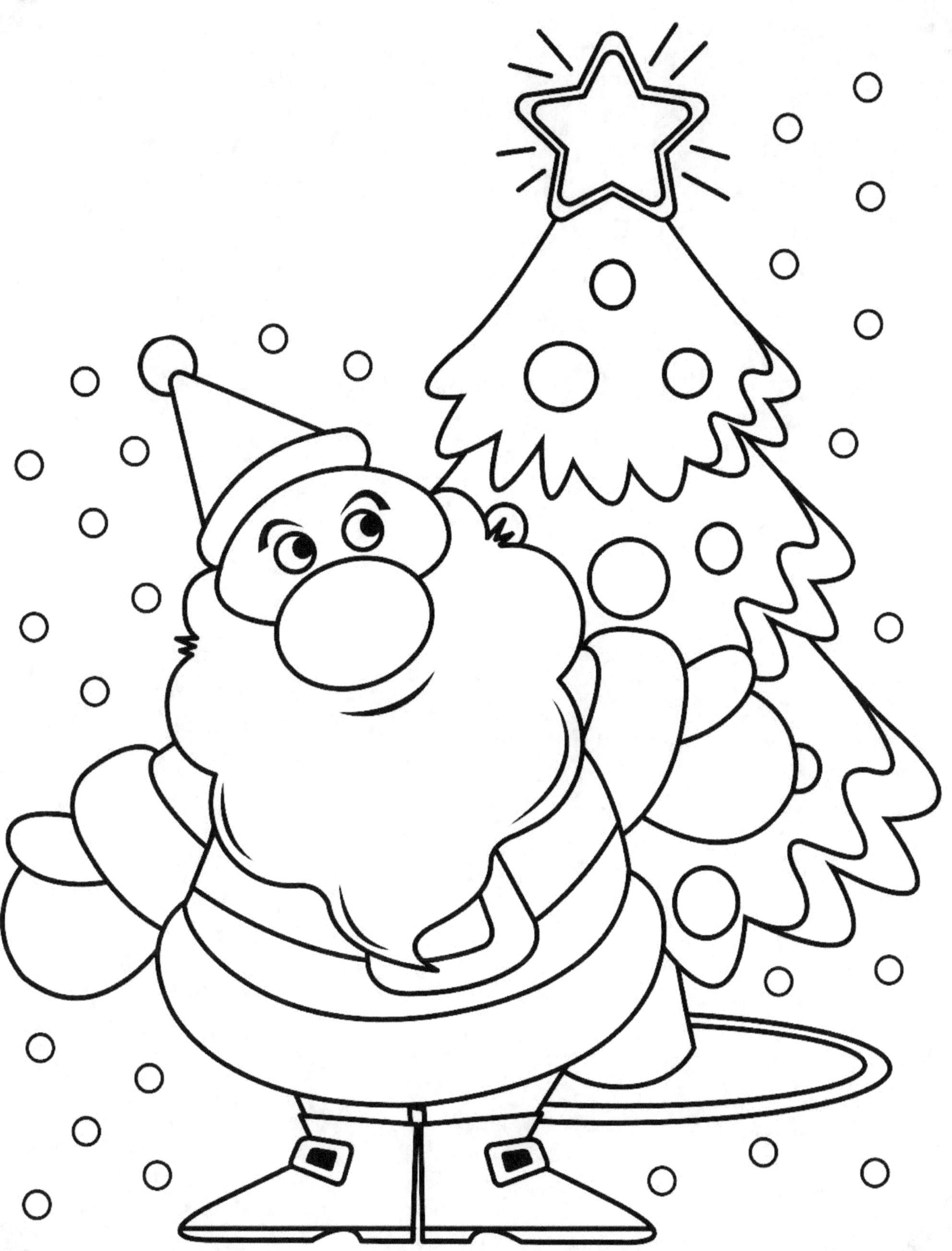

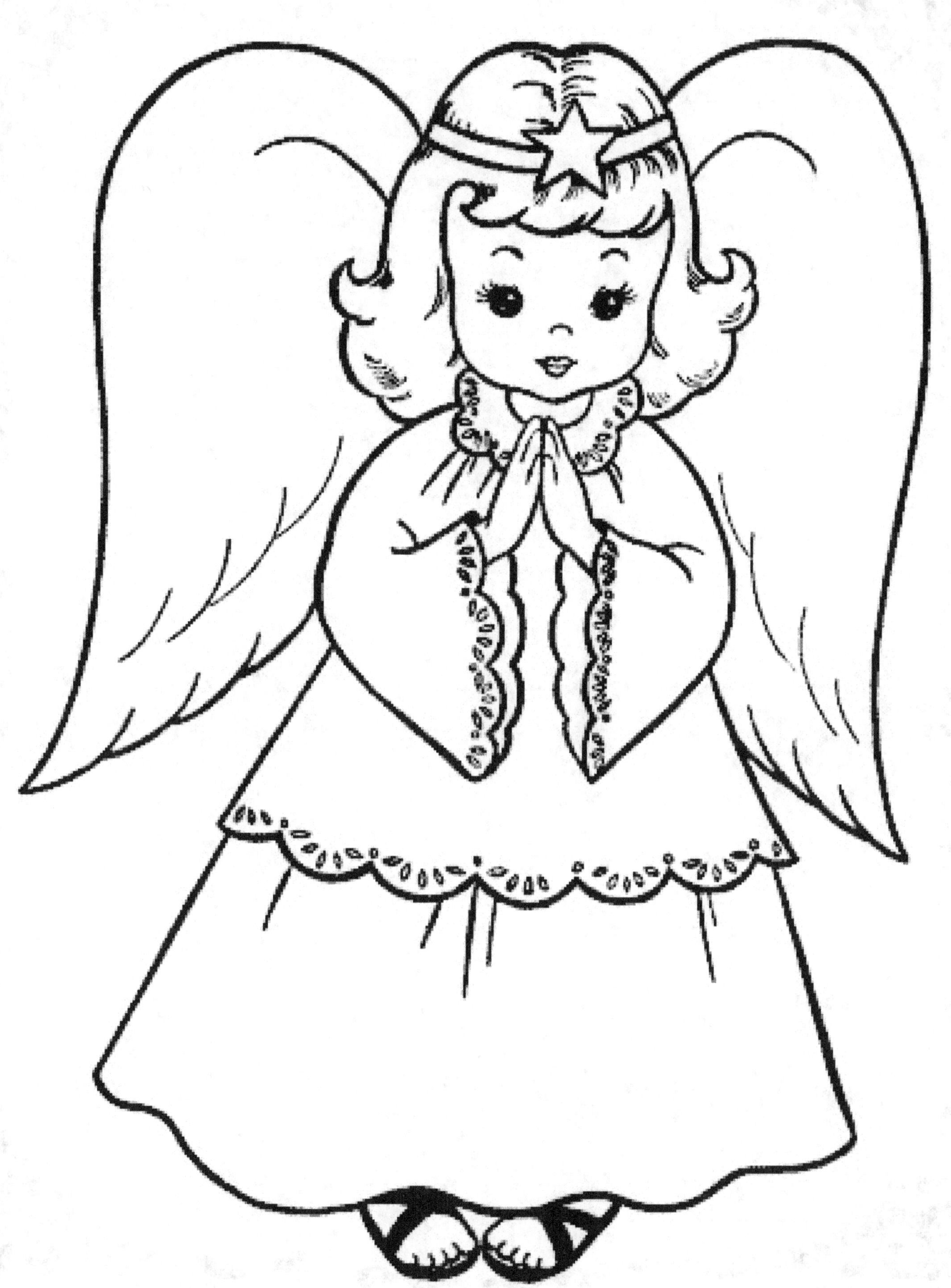

www.ingramcontent.com/pod-product-compliance
Lightning Source LLC
Chambersburg PA
CBHW081444250726
48662CB00009B/2939